Theraplay *& Other Plays*

Other works by Christopher Bollas

Non-fiction
The Shadow of the Object
Forces of Destiny
Being a Character
Perche' Edipo?
Cracking Up
The New Informants (with David Sundelson)
The Mystery of Things
Hysteria
Free Association

Fiction
Dark at the End of the Tunnel
I Have Heard the Mermaids Singing

Theraplay *& Other Plays*
Christopher Bollas

With an introduction by Anthony Molino

Free Association Books

FA^B

Published in the United Kingdom 2006
by Free Association Books
57 Warren Street
London
W1T 5NR
www.fabooks.com

If you wish to apply for amateur or professional performing
rights please write to Prairie Productions, P.O. Box 173,
Tolna, North Dakota 58380, USA
and email the author at
theraplay@christopherbollas.com

British Library Cataloguing in Publication Data
A catalogue record of this book is available from the British Library

Designed by Charlie Smith Design
Produced by Bookchase Limited
Printed and bound in the United Kingdom

ISBN 1-85343-968-1

Acknowledgements
Thanks to Sarah Nettleton and Robert Timms
for their editorial assistance

Contents

Introduction

We cannot take a single step beyond our own impotence; outside those walls I feel sick and giddy. If the wall is no longer there, the gulf opens at my feet and I am seized with dizziness.

Eugène Ionesco

Ionesco. Beckett. Pinter. Pirandello. Dürrenmatt. Signposts of a century of theatre, where chronology, or time itself, verges on collapse even as it stands still. 'I am at an age when you grow ten years older in one year, when an hour is only a few minutes long and you cannot even note the passing quarters,' writes Ionesco in his *Fragments of a Journal*. Dali's melted clocks. Petrified. Godot has not yet arrived, nor has the Author ever materialised. Existentialism. 'One must imagine Sisyphus happy.' Ambivalence of being. Mourn? – or celebrate? – the exit of the King. By the way: Word has it God is dead. Theatre of the absurd, living. Still. Maybe. In the collapse of a century. In the black hole that inaugurates, sweeps in, sucks up another before it even gets off the ground. Zero. 911? No, more. The Catastrophe beyond. Good and Evil melded, entwined, entangled. Confused. Osama. O'mama! No more. Nothing. And the tragedy is real. Everywhere. Prefigurations: Orwell, Giacometti. Or, perhaps the work of an arsonist, who burns the plays of a young man, who, traumatised, stays silent – sort of – for forty years. Silence. 'Hello darkness, my old friend . . .' Our past present. Imperfected. All (all?) in these works by Christopher Bollas. Who?

More, later, about the author's identity. I-dentity. Ego's teeth. Its bite. While the plays here can tear at flesh – of the body, mind or soul (which feels better, more real today?) – the characters are often stripped bare of any defining I-ness. Suffice it to list some names: Aldo Hurt ('Theraplay'); Manuel Dirsk ('Apply Within'); the Flounts ('Piecemeal'). What's there to flaunt, in blank, often windowless spaces where the End is everywhere in the air? Mindless, gasping survivors of some osmotic Catastrophe, they operate like an alexithymic army of post-human beings, riddled, hardly but thankfully, by the fallout of the complexities of once-human relations. Ontic vestiges, bits and pieces of life as we know it. 'I am the walrus . . .' Damage control. Gagging automatons enshrined on the altars of Role and Function. Malevich gone mad. Orwell's great-grandchildren. Who hurt, nonetheless, unthinking, unknowing. Schizoid emanations of the Elephant Man. This much, strangely, we do feel, as readers, as audience. In settings that defy locale and practically preclude any ordinary capacity for empathy and identification, we, nonetheless, *feel.* Something. Something nagging, fastidious, worming. Burning. Then we imagine or see. Them. Cringed. Singed. Did I mention Giacometti? Read 'Old Friends' (my favourite, along with 'Apply Within'), and see, sense, the sculptor's wrinkled, writhing, desperate creations.

Double-take. A job applicant in 'Apply Within' thinks suffusing the workplace with Rachmaninoff is the key to his hiring. A woman strips, convinced the job's hers. Another insists that only by attending to the dying can the job be secured and ennobled. Florence Nightingale, you're the next contestant in the 'Save your Skin and Screw the World' sweepstakes! Since hilarity somehow seeps through the cracks of bleak scenarios in all of these works, it's only fair to say that, as with all theatre, these black comedies await transposition from text to stage: to fester fully and fizz to fruition. In search of an audience – which they will find – they conjure up, and indeed demand, rabid eyes and hungry ears. And, now and then, hearty laughs.

Bollas, Christopher, b. 1943. Close to the age, I'd guess, when Ionesco was writing in his notebooks about time flying and had death gnawing at his mind. Psychoanalyst. Author. Two stark, comic novels: one, *Dark at the End of the Tunnel*, on death and dying and living in spite of it all (Camus *docet*); the other, *I Have Heard the Mermaids Singing*, a quasi-celebration of depression, a jeremiad against the pharmaceutical industry and its pandemic panaceas, mediated by the surreal, harrowing apparition in a psychoanalyst's office of a terrorist seeking help to carry out his deadly mission. Dynamite stuff. Baghdad in Britain. Prophetic, sadly. Funny how this all reminds me of a poem I translated years ago, lines that read:

> The themes too aren't all that different
> in fact, there's only one theme,
> the theme itself. Again.
>
> Valerio Magrelli, 'Nearsights'

Bollas's theme? Humanity, or the threat of its loss. Our loss. Staged. 'All over the world.' Something to do, maybe, with what he lost, in that fire forty years ago, a fire that silenced a genre in him for four decades but gave us all, for many of those years, some of the most vivid, compelling visions of the theatrical space that is a psychoanalysis. Not just Oedipus, blinded, lost somewhere between Thebes and Colonus, or Hamlet brooding over a skull, driving Ophelia insane. Live theatre. Breathing. Record runs, years on end. How many times a week? Really, really absurd. Crazy-making, contaminating, hazardous to normotic standards of health.

The consulting room informs these plays, and is both their germ and their theatrical counterpoint. A place for play that is *not* theraplay, alien to the values of a world where Aldo Hurts get 'resexualised' and 'reprofessionalised'. Play, theatre, that will not forsake hope. In Bollas's words: 'Psychoanalysis *is* a theatre of the absurd, in a way, a totally asymmetrical relationship, where there are no heroes, only anti-heroes, where nobody comes out idealised but everybody, patient and analyst alike, is humbled by his or her *human* limitations.' Which is maybe why these ominous works close out on an altogether happy note. A farce. Really. *À la* Marx Brothers. About an analyst, Dr Scarf, and a New Mexican named Wellbird. (Where else would a happy American pecker come from? Wellbird: 'D.H. Lawrence, meet Georgia O'Keefe.') Trust me, Bollas does know how to laugh. And how not to take himself, his profession, and maybe even the whole lot of us, too seriously. Not always, at least. Curtain time. Enjoy the show.

Anthony Molino

Theraplay

A play in four acts

Cast

Aldo Hurt

Julie

Angela

Sarah

Beth

Gayle

Veronica

First Man

Second Man

Voice

Courier

Act one

A drab meeting room with worn furniture: a small settee, a low coffee table and four or five chairs. There is a door stage right. When the curtain opens, the room is unoccupied and it remains so for thirty seconds.

The door flies open suddenly and Aldo Hurt rushes into the room. He is dressed in a cheap, crumpled blue linen suit and is carrying a tattered briefcase in his left hand. He has a rather scruffy plum-coloured scarf over his shoulder. Except at the end of the play, he will have his scarf with him throughout, and will play with it in various ways.

Aldo   *(in a panic, as though talking to a room full of people)* I'm so sorry for . . . *(pauses, looks around, realises he is alone but can barely believe this)* . . . being late . . . ?

He looks around carefully again, as if he cannot trust his perception; then he twirls round twice, as if this will shake his mind and he will find the room full of people after all.

       So, I'm not late then? *(pauses)* Not so. I suppose . . . *(still not convinced)* that I must be the first one! *(looks around again, gets down on his knees to look under the coffee table, then jumps to his feet in glee)* I am here first. *(pumps the air with his fist)* Whew! *(pauses, looks at the door, and adopts an officious tone)* Let's see. This IS Room 228, isn't it?

Suddenly quite anxious, he drops the briefcase, grips the scarf in his hand and exits through the door, which he shuts behind him. He returns after a few seconds.

Yep . . . 228. 228 it is. I'm in the right room. Don't know where the others could be. But I'm here. In the right room. *(during a long pause, he looks around as if studying the empty space)* Well, what should I do? Stand here a bit longer? Sit down? It might look presumptuous. *(stiffening, pointing with his right hand to the settee)* 'Oh, it's you, Hurt, sitting down already? Don't bother to get up.' *(winces, as if in pain)* Awww . . . that would look awful. *(sits down, puts his head in his hands and speaks in a low voice)* The others are probably just on their way, maybe about to . . . *(pauses, looks at the closed door)* . . . any moment they're going to open . . . *(keeps looking at the door, concentrating on it, and is silent for twenty seconds)* Nope? Not yet then? *(pauses)* Well, the important thing is that I'm here. I'M HERE. It cannot be said that I am not here. Ha! 'Where is Hurt? Not here yet? Oh dear: late, we must assume.' *(gets up suddenly and prances to a space near the centre of the room)* No, I'm here: right behind you. Actually, I was here first! *(gloating, he walks slowly and deliberately around the room, singing in a low voice)* I'm here. I'm here. I'm here. I'm here. *(stops suddenly)* Maybe I'll just have a look at the memo.

He sits on a chair and opens his briefcase. Papers spill out onto the floor and over the coffee table.

Oh, for God's sake! For God's sake! Can't you do anything right? Papers everywhere. All kinds of papers. What papers? Oh my God, not those papers, they mustn't see those papers, no one must see those papers, for God's sake hurry – pick them up. *(he mashes the papers into balls and plunges them into his briefcase in a panic, before snapping it shut)* Oh, thank God. Thank God. Imagine. No. Don't imagine. Just calm down. Say it again. Say it again and say it calmly. Just . . . calm . . . down. You are calming down. Say it again. Calm . . . down . . . That's good. *(pauses)* Now you are calm. There was no need to panic like that.

Unless . . . no, don't go there. No one is here. It's okay.
You are here, they aren't, and you have done all the right
things. Nothing is wrong. Now, open your briefcase . . .
Sit down first. *(returns to the settee)* Let's see, one ball at a
time. Open up, little ball! *(he uncurls each ball of paper in
turn, peeking inside)* Nope. Nope. Not THAT ONE. *(in a
childish voice)* That's a bad piece of paper. *(opens another
ball)* OH HO! Now that's really very, very bad. You stay in
there. Don't you dare come out again. *(opens a third ball)*
Now, this looks about right. There you are, you lovely
little thing. Let's see what you have to say. *(he flattens the
crumpled paper out on the coffee table)* You say 'Meeting at
The Centre, 12th of November, Room 228, 4.30 p.m.'
and that's right where I am and it's . . . it's *(pauses, looks at
his watch and panics)* Oh blast. The time! What time is it?
Oh my God, MY WATCH IS BROKEN. Oh hell. You've
done it again. Again. You've bungled things. You've missed
the meeting. How could you have done it? Well? Well?
(slowly) How . . . could . . . you . . . have . . . done . . . it?
*(walks quickly around the room in a goose-step, raising his
arm in a Hitler salute)* Heil Moron! Heil Moron! Heil
Moron! Heil Moron! Heil Moron!

*He collapses into a chair, covering his face with the scarf. He breathes
heavily for some time and gradually calms down. Then suddenly he becomes
agitated.*

But what time is it? Your watch is broken. What does it
say? When did it break? 11.45 a.m.? When was that? How
did you think it was 4.30, when it says 11.45? What sort
of mistake is that? Never mind. Figure that out later.
Later? How do you know the meeting is over? It could be
that it hasn't started yet! Maybe it hasn't started! Maybe
you really are early! Maybe you really were first . . . but . . .
how early? Just . . . CALM DOWN, say it calmly . . . No,
I can't, there isn't enough time, or there's too much time; I
will calm down later, I am calm enough anyway. I just
have to look at my . . . I just have to figure out the time.

That's it. I have to figure out the time. It is either before 4.30 or after 4.30. Your watch stopped at 11.45. Where were you? What were you doing? I've had lunch. That's right. What time? Well, I don't know, I don't know: the usual time, I'm sure. About 1. Then what did you do? I wrote two letters and did some admin. Then I phoned Hexter and we talked for . . . for? . . . for about about 15 minutes. So what time is it now, at that time? Let's see, um, 1 o'clock, two letters, half an hour each, that's 2 o'clock. No, you forgot lunch! Lunch, then letters. *(repeats very fast)* Okay okay okay okay okay okay okay. Now. Lunch finishes at 1.30 – that's good – always hate eating in that shitty café anyway, just grab a sandwich and shove it down the pipe, so now, it's 2.30 after the letters, then the phone call to . . . WAIT A MINUTE, the drains man! Oh shit, of course. He came with his estimate. Ah, let's see, how long was that – HURRY UP – I am, I am, let's see, it was about, he walked in, opened up the cover in the bathroom, we talked about holidays, it was probably – probably half an hour. ADD THIRTY MINUTES. Yes, to what? TO . . . TO . . . Calm yourself. Where were you? I was at . . . at . . . 2.30, then the drains guy, that takes me to 3. Then the call to Thingamajig? Yes, that was only, um, fifteen minutes. SO? SO? So I must have . . . this was all finished at about 3.30 at the latest. THAT'S IT, YOU'RE SURE? Yes, I am. I'm sure. And how long did it take to get here: max? Just max. Ah, 45 minutes. YOU'RE SURE? Yes. Yes. I'm sure.

By this time he is jumping up and down, running round the room, and he fails to notice the door open. A man in a black suit stands in the doorway, watching. He will appear later as the First Man.

I'm sure! I'm sure! I'm so happy I'm sure. *(sings to the tune of 'I am pretty, oh so pretty')* I'm so sure, I'm so sure, I'm so sure, so sure, so sure, so sure.

As he dances exultantly round the room he passes the man, who then shuts the door and disappears. Aldo is ten feet past the door before he realises what he thinks he has seen. Suddenly he is aware of what he is doing and saying. He slows to a walk and speaks calmly with artificial audibility.

I'm sure the floor of this room is perfectly fine, and any anxieties on the part of the Building Committee are ill-founded. Why it should fall to me to have to repeatedly inspect this building, I don't know. But someone has to do it. So here I am, pacing round this room, yet again having to test the soundness of the floor because The Centre can't – apparently *(nervous, derisive laugh)* – get anyone to fix it for them.

He gives a quick glance over his shoulder to see where the man is, and he continues to talk, obviously to a person whom he assumes is within earshot.

Floors, walls, ceilings, light fixtures, paintwork: it all has to be inspected by someone. Doesn't it? *(glances quickly over his right shoulder)* And doors, of course, doors need checking.

He picks up his briefcase and rushes out the door. He is gone for about thirty seconds, then walks calmly back into the room, without the briefcase, closes the door, and sits down. After a pause, he stands up again, walks into the middle of the room and stares fixedly at the door, rather as one might gaze at a painting.

Well, I know there was someone there. I saw him, or her. Not a her. It was definitely a him. No need to play round with rhetoric here. It was a person. I saw him as sure as I see that door. Or these chairs. Or my briefcase. MY BRIEFCASE! Where is my briefcase? What have I done with it?

He searches frantically around the room, throwing the cushions off the settee, overturning the chairs, looking under the coffee table.

Oh my God! Oh my God! Oh my God! *(runs out of the room, then re-enters thirty seconds later)* Well, it's gone. It's just gone. It's gone. You have to accept it. But what could have happened to it? It can't have just walked out of the room all by itself, can it? You must have taken it with you when you left the room . . . But why would I have done that? Whatever for? What possible reason would I have had to remove my briefcase? I mean, it's not as if I was going to a meeting, is it? Or did I think I was going to another meeting? Did I? Did I go out of Room 228 to attend another meeting? Wouldn't I remember that? Not today, you wouldn't. Everything is going wrong today. You could lose your mind today and never find it. Hah! That was funny, wasn't it! You could lose your mind and never find it. Hah! Hah! *(utters a forced laugh, followed by a long pause)* What does it mean to lose your mind? And if you do, then what? It's gone missing. What do you do, report it to the police? 'Hello, 999. I'm calling to report the loss of my mind. I don't know. I don't know what's happened to it; but it's missing. It was here and now it is gone.'

He collapses onto the settee and is silent for half a minute.

What did happen to your briefcase? You don't know, do you? *(jumps up in alarm)* HELP! HELP! OH GOD, ALL THOSE PAPERS IN MY BRIEFCASE.

He walks quickly round in a tight circle, his arms wrapped around himself tightly, then stops, bends over and screams.

OH BLAST, BLAST, BLAST, BLAST!

He collapses onto the settee again and is silent, as if trying to control his breathing. Then he talks to himself in a lowered voice, seemingly trying to reassure and control himself at the same time.

There is NOTHING that you can do about it. It is gone. The papers are gone. Things go away. Disappear. Important things. You have to accept what has happened. And you have to remember, that now, right now, there is just nothing, just nothing at all, that you can do about it. *(pauses)* Cut your losses. Yeah, sure, cut your losses! Just cut them! *(pauses, looking up at the ceiling)* This is not a good day. Just not a good day. *(sits forward, elbows on his knees, pulling himself together)* Anyway! At any moment a member of The Organisation could step through that door and you have to settle yourself. They will expect you to take part in their discussion; to make some sort of creative contribution to what they're talking about. So, why not give THAT some thought? This is a good idea. Um . . . let's see . . . the topic of the meeting. Well. What is the topic of the meeting? You know, I don't think I know. It was something about, about . . . well of course, it's probably in the bloody briefcase, but that's lost. Don't go there, JUST DON'T GO BACK THERE. *(pauses)* So. Wasn't it to do with the idea of 'moving on'? I think that's it, the idea of moving on. Hey, good, you've got it. Moving on. Time to move on. So . . . good. And so . . . what do you suppose . . . they have in mind? What ideas can you come up with that have to do with moving on? *(holds up his left hand, fingers spread out)* Well, there are five reasons why we are moving on. First, we have to, because of the crisis in which we now find ourselves. *(looks around, as if someone is listening between each of these statements)* Second, this crisis is a result of a failure to move on earlier – in our past – so we must do it now. Third, if we don't move on now, we will lose out. Fourth, we must move in order to adopt a new spirit, to get out of our rut. Fifth, we must transform bad circumstances into new and hopeful possibilities. Hey! Hey! Hey! WE MUST TRANSFORM BAD CIRCUMSTANCES INTO NEW AND HOPEFUL POSSIBILITIES. *(pumps the air)* That's great. They are going to love that. What a ring to it, eh? Great ring. You can play with it, turn it around. We MUST transform. Or, WE must transform. Or, we must TRANSFORM. Damn, this is so good, so good. It's a great statement. And it ends on a positive note. So . . . so . . . where the heck is everybody, then? It must be 4.40 at least by now. I'm ready to go, up and running, cheerful –

even though it's been a shitty day so far. But hey! Apply your own medicine, mate: you must transform bad circumstances into new and hopeful possibilities. You've broken your watch and lost your briefcase, but not only is it not the end of the world, it's actually the beginning of something hopeful. This is a transformational moment. Something really good is about to happen.

He pauses, as if listening to some sound from beyond the door, but there is silence.

But look, something good did just happen, didn't it? You were in a really horrid state and you had a good idea, it's given you something for the meeting, and so maybe that's enough. Maybe you don't need much more. Things are looking up. I think I'll just go check out the action – see what's up.

He exits, closing the door behind him. The lights go down and the coffee table and two chairs are removed by a man who enters from the side of the stage or from the audience, and whom the audience will later recognise as the Courier. Aldo re-enters the room.

What the . . . ! What's this? Where . . . where did the . . . the . . . the . . . what do you call that . . . the coffee table . . . where did the coffee table go? And a chair is gone. No . . . two chairs are gone. What? How long were you gone? One minute? Just out into the hall, round the corner, past the abandoned coffee bar, out into the corridor near the lifts, then straight back. How could this have happened? Someone just came in and got rid of this stuff? How? I mean, like where? I would have seen them, don't you think?

He stares desperately out into the audience and addresses them directly.

I mean, did anyone see anything disappear? Did anyone notice? How did these things just leave? This is not possible, is it? Is this my problem? Am I meant . . . ? It doesn't make sense. Things don't just disappear like that, do they? There has to be a reason for something like this.

There just has to be. But what could it be? *(crosses his arms pensively, calming down)* There has to be a logical explanation for this kind of thing. Just because I didn't see the coffee table and the chairs leaving, it doesn't mean that they didn't go for a perfectly good reason. This is part of your problem. If you can't see the reason why something happens, you panic because you assume, somehow, that it has something to do with you. Simply because you personally didn't see the chairs and table disappear, you panic, while of course, there is a reason for this: they didn't just walk out of their own accord! So, let's think. How did they disappear? Well . . . first of all, you're probably wrong in your assumption. Simply because they're no longer here, it doesn't mean that they've disappeared. They still exist – they've just been relocated. That's it, RE-LOCATED. That's what has happened. And why? Why relocated? Well, I'd have no idea about that, would I? In a situation like this, it's not for me to determine intention or motivation, only to note that something has happened. Certain things have been relocated. I have no need to know more than that! *(pauses, hands on his head)* Well, you say that they've been relocated, but actually they may well have been destroyed, so really you can't come up with a term like 'relocated' just because it makes you feel better. The 'feel-better factor'. No, that's a cop-out. The chairs and table may have been stolen and sold, they may have been taken and dumped in the rubbish and are now destroyed. I mean, clearly lots of things go missing and we don't know where they are. People disappear. Think of Chile, Argentina – people go missing. Death. Everyone dies, so they go missing. It's funny, isn't it, but you never actually see people die, do you? It's not like we're all out there walking on the street and every now and then we see someone fall over dead. You'd think with the rate of death – I mean, probably every few seconds someone dies – that you'd see all sorts of people dying on the way to work, dying in cafés, in parks while flying kites, on the banks of the river while fishing, at the theatre . . . But how many times do we see this? What does it look like, eh? How do the dying fall? Well, walking, it must be like this.

He veers off to his right, grabs the wall and crumples before it. He is still and lifeless for some time; then he gets up slowly.

Wow, that was something. And flying a kite, how do the dying look flying a kite? *(holds his hand up in the air, as if holding a string)* How do you die, flying a kite? When you're with your kid, your son, who is eight years old, how do you look? *(clutches his throat, looks around below him and falls to the ground, almost sobbing)* I can't breathe, I can't breathe. I'm so sorry. 'Daddy is dying.' You'll be okay. Daddy loves you. Call for help. Tell Mum I love her. I am so sorry.

He continues to cry for some time, with the sobbing slowly becoming softer and rhythmic, like an infant's; then he is still. He sits up and rubs his eyes.

God, what a day. What a bewildering day this is. It's all just so odd. No idea what to make of this. *(gets to his feet slowly and sits in a chair, gradually recovering)* Oh well, anyway, we don't see people dying in the streets or flying their kites. They're all off dying in the hospitals, then, aren't they? Got to be. That's where they die. That's why we don't see any dying on the streets or in the parks or at the theatre. They get to the hospital in time to die there, and if they find they've made a mistake and they're not dying after all, the hospital kills them anyway. What's that? 87,000 people died last year due to hospital error! Bleeding hell!

He laughs loudly, then for a while he stares quietly ahead of him, exhausted and still. Suddenly he doubles over, apparently in acute pain.

OW! OW! OW! . . . Oh God, I'm starved! I'm thirsty! I haven't had anything to eat. It hurts. Oh God! I need food. I have to drink. My throat is parched. My insides are totally dried out. The pain . . . oh help . . . the pain in my stomach, the gnawing, kneading pain. I have to eat. I'm starving! *(pauses, puts his forefingers to his temples, as if forcing himself to concentrate)* Why am I so hungry? Didn't I eat? And drink? Didn't I just have lunch? *(releases his head)* You remember, you remember you had lunch? Didn't you? Maybe you didn't, maybe you just think you did. Oh God, I must have skipped it. I thought I crammed down a sandwich at the café, but now I know that's not true. I missed lunch, I missed my own lunch, I missed it because that fool from the drains company showed up when I was supposed to go for my lunch and I couldn't leave and then I had to rush here, that's why I'm dying of thirst and hunger. But I had breakfast, that should have kept me from . . . I . . . did I have breakfast? *(bangs his head gently with his fist)* Did I have my tea and toast? I always do. I always have my tea and toast, my brown toast with real butter and jam on it. Real strawberry jam, thick, piled high on my toast, my two pieces of toast, with lots of strawberry jam and my tea, my hot cup of tea, with just the right amount of milk in it, my toast and my tea, I have them, I always do. That should stop this pain. *(doubles over again with a mild yell)* God, it's so painful, why? Why so much pain? Why in my gut? I've had my tea and toast. I have had them. Haven't I? Haven't I? *(looks round the room, as if he will see some evidence of his breakfast)* I mean, I can't have forgotten my tea and toast. Oh God. God, please help me. I think I have. I think I have forgotten. I think I have forgotten to have my tea and toast. I think I must have. I have no memory of it. I . . . I . . . can't recall it. I was in the kitchen, but I don't remember washing my knife, drying it, and putting it away. I must have run out of the house because I was late. I must have got up late and rushed out before I had my tea and toast.

He falls to the floor and crumples up in a semi-foetal position, sometimes kicking his feet. He is yelling and is panicked.

> I'VE HAD NOTHING TO EAT ALL DAY. I AM STARVING. I AM STARVING. I AM NOT GOING TO SURVIVE. I CAN'T STAY HERE A MINUTE LONGER. I HAVE TO GET OUT OF HERE. MEETING OR NO MEETING, I HAVE TO GET OUT OF HERE. THE PAIN IS UNBEARABLE. I HAVE TO PUT SOMETHING IN MY STOMACH. I HAVE TO HAVE WATER. WATER, I HAVE TO HAVE WATER. I HAVE TO HAVE WATER.

He springs to his feet and runs out of the room, but immediately rushes back in and shuts the door. He walks over to the settee and sits down slowly, now speaking in a soft, distant voice.

> There's no water out there. You looked. You have to calm yourself down. You are raging with hunger and dying of thirst, but you can't leave. You have to stay here and attend the meeting. Everything depends on it. Your position. Your future. Everything. So you must just be still. Be still. Meditate. Control your breathing.

He gets up and, in a rather seamless motion, sits on the floor in the middle of the room and contorts himself into some kind of ill-formed lotus position. He is still for a moment, then he hears a cough in the hall on the other side of the door and is startled.

> Oh. *(pauses)* Oh. Hello? *(pauses)* Hello? *(anxious, not sure what to do)* Is there someone there? Hello? The meeting is in this room.

He waits and listens, leaning his body forward.

> Hello?

The lights go out.

Act two

Aldo is lying on the settee, asleep. Muffled voices can be heard in the distance, and as he hears them he wakes up, opening his eyes. After a few seconds it becomes clear that it is the sound of a group of women outside the door, talking and laughing loudly.

The door bursts open and six women enter, each carrying several shopping bags from the high street. They are in their late twenties or early thirties, rather girly, bubbly, their gestures confident and exaggerated – in stark contrast to Aldo, who is in shock, overwhelmed by their numbers and their bravado. They see Aldo but take almost no notice of him. Their remarks to him are casual, offhand and somewhat affectionate, but seem intended to keep him outside their group.

Julie	Yeah, well she would say that, wouldn't she? I mean, if you use dark grey eyeshadow with black eyeliner, of course it makes your eyes look small. But she's just jealous. She can't take it. But you know what you should do?
Angela	Like what?
Julie	Well, you use blue or purple. Not grey. That way your eyes aren't small and you look cool.
Gayle	Yeah, but we do have small eyes.
Julie	In comparison to what?
Gayle	*(looks away, uncomfortable)* Well . . . you know.

Julie	I know what? *(looks around at the group with a falsely quizzical expression)*
Gayle	I mean . . . you know . . .
Julie	What?
Gayle	Well, since things have gone wrong . . . you can't say we look the same.
Beth	We?
Gayle	I think our faces have changed.
Veronica	What, you mean, cosmetics?
Gayle	No, I mean, things have changed. Our faces are different. I don't look at people any more. I look at the ground.
Aldo	*(in the background, almost imperceptibly)* The ground?
Julie	Come on, Gayle!
Gayle	It's just that I don't think we're as wide open as we once were. But maybe this is just rubbish.
Beth	No, Gayle. You're just on another wavelength. *(turns back to Julie)* Where were we, Julie?
Sarah	Yeah, so Julie, what else did she say? It sounds AMAZING!
Julie	Oh, she's always going on about something, isn't she?
Beth	Go on, what did she say?
Sarah	She said the reason that Barbara's make-up slid off last night was that she had over-moisturised her face.
Julie	Yeah, well tell us something we don't know. I mean, Barbara's face is always slipping off!
All (except Julie and Aldo)	Ooooh, Julie, that was nasty!

Gayle   Well, what can Barbara do to stop her face slipping off? I feel mine's doing that right now. I look in the mirror and see it change day to day. Sometimes I have to hold it in both hands, very hard, to stop it from sliding off my head.

The other women are disturbed and ignore Gayle, but Aldo sits up slightly and looks at her.

Aldo   *(again unheard by the group)* Yes. I can't find my face. It changes every day. I try to keep it steady but . . .

Julie   *(loudly, to the others, as if Gayle had not just spoken)* Just use a light moisturiser with a non-transferable base.

Angela   That makes sense!

Julie   Yes, makes sense, doesn't it?

Julie takes a bottle out of one of her shopping bags.

Sarah   Oh Julie, is that Valva?

Julie   You bet it is.

Sarah   Oh, can I have a look?

Julie   *(teasing)* Well . . .

Sarah   Oh come on, can I? Please, please, PLEASE!

Julie throws her the bottle, and in a rather graceful move walks towards the door.

Julie   I'll be right back in a mo – we need more chairs. *(exits)*

Sarah   Oh, it's so cool. It's got Nutrilight deep-acting oil.

Beth   Nutrilight?

Sarah   It's so cool.

Gayle   I think I tried that, but I don't know about it. I don't know about trying anything any more. What's the point? The men are . . .

Aldo sits up straight to listen, then slumps back down again.

17

Beth   Forget the men, Gayle. We're not here to talk about that. *(angrily)* Just concentrate on what we've bought, OKAY?

Gayle sits in a chair and slumps slightly so she is in somewhat the same position as Aldo is on the settee.

Sarah   I don't know, but I know it's cool. It says it's instantly absorbed into the hair, from top to bottom, from root to tip, and it calms you.

Julie   *(from the doorway)* Can you help me?

She is trying to enter, carrying two chairs, and she can't negotiate the door. Aldo gets up in a flash and takes one of the chairs from her hand.

             Thanks, sweetie.

Beth takes the chair from Aldo and she and Julie arrange all the chairs in a circle. Aldo is left standing where Beth took the chair from him. Julie heads back to the door.

             Back in another mo. *(exits)*

Angela   I think Nutrilight is great, anyway. Where's my lipstick?

Beth   I'm afraid, Angela darling, your problem isn't going to be solved by lipstick.

Angela   Huh?

Beth   You know, your lipstick is always fading away and you're always reapplying, you know what I mean?

Angela   *(embarrassed)* You've noticed that?

Beth   Sure . . . what you've got to do, love, is you've got to prep your skin with powder.

Gayle   Or concealer, I think.

Beth   Yeah, or concealer – you see, that way it stays on longer and you don't have to keep reaching into your pouch and putting more on.

Sarah   Yeah, it sort of cakes up when you do that.

Julie re-enters the room backwards, pulling a coffee table.

Julie   Did I hear someone say 'cake'? Oh yummy! I'm famished. Any help here?

Aldo comes to her rescue and together they carry the table towards the centre of the room. But they can't easily co-ordinate their efforts: they move the table too far to the right, then over-correct to the left. Seeing the problem, the other women look mildly alarmed.

        Ooops.

Aldo   Sorry!

Julie   There we go . . . ooops.

Aldo   Ah, uh . . . oh . . .

Julie   There . . . no . . . let's . . .

Aldo   Sorry . . .

All   Watch out for the chair!
(except Julie
and Aldo)

Julie drops her end of the table onto the floor, leaving Aldo holding his end. Julie is frustrated, impatient to end the fiasco.

Julie   That's fine, there's a nice chappy, thanks so much.

Aldo puts his end of the table down and walks backwards towards a lone chair, which he plops into. Beth and Julie bring the table to centre stage. The women quickly arrange cakes and juices, with exclamations of 'yummy!', 'this looks good!', and so on.

Aldo   *(so softly that the women cannot hear)* I'm starved.

Sarah   Did you know that drinking makes your skin go all dry?

Gayle   Is that a man?

Julie	Yes.
Gayle	A man – a real man?
Julie	Don't make this complicated, Gayle.
Gayle	Well, it's just that . . .
Beth	What?
Gayle	I haven't seen many men lately.
Veronica	Well . . . go to the library and look them up!

They all laugh at Gayle – heartily but unkindly. Aldo is in the background in a dissociated state, taking it in, but not yet a real part of the scene.

Beth	So drinking dries up your skin?
Sarah	Yeah, that's why women in their forties start to look all scaly; they've been drinking too much.
Veronica	*(preoccupied)* Oh, I couldn't stand that.
Julie	What?
Veronica	Having to give up drink.
Aldo	*(a bit louder, so they now hear him)* I'm so thirsty I could die. *(the women ignore him)*
Julie	You don't have to give up drink. There's a cure.
All (except Julie and Aldo)	WHAT?
Julie	When you drink your glass of wine, for each sip of booze, have a sip of water. The water counteracts the dehydrating effects of alcohol. It's simple and it works!
Veronica	Thank God I don't have to give up drink.
Beth	That's fantastic!

Aldo	*(louder still, but the women continue to ignore him)* I'm dying of starvation. I have to have something to drink.
Sarah	You know what?
Aldo and the other women	What?
Sarah	Forget all about collagen injections – you don't need them. And anyway, who can afford stuff like that? What you do is, you get this thing called 'Mouthoff', it's a gel, and you plump your lips, you put it on, and your lips increase in size. It's really great!
Gayle	How does it work?
Sarah	Simple, it increases the blood flow to the lips. The lips swell, and – presto – you've got sexy lips, and without collagen.
Veronica	Sounds pretty cool to me.
Aldo	Look, I'm really hungry.
Julie	*(looking over her shoulder at Aldo)* Oh, hi love. Really?
Aldo	Really.
Julie	I mean, for real?
Aldo	Really.
Gayle	It's not like a metaphor or something?
Aldo	A metaphor?
Angela	She means, like a way of saying, 'Hey girls, you know . . . I'm really hungry for . . .' *(becomes embarrassed)* You know what I mean . . .
Beth	Yeah, like hungry for company, or hungry for conversation, or hungry for ideas. You know . . . hungry.
Aldo	No, I mean I'm really hungry.

Veronica	You don't look hungry. Anyway, how could you be hungry?
Aldo	Well, I don't think I've had any lunch or breakfast, and I'm starving and thirsty.
Julie	Yeah, well, OKAY – we can spare a banana – anyone seen the bananas? – and we have half a juice left. But I mean … why? Couldn't you just go out and get something to eat?

Beth reaches into her bag for a banana and a juice and passes it to Julie, who holds it, about to give it to Aldo.

Aldo	I can't leave the room. I am here for the meeting.

Julie hands him the banana and the juice, which he takes like a shy animal, coming up to it and then grabbing it quickly, before retreating to his chair, where he immediately throws all the juice down his throat and then crams the banana into his mouth.

Veronica	Ah, poor thing. Poor guy, you really were very hungry.
Gayle	Poor love.
Julie	Yeah, poor guy, huh?
Sarah	Definitely.
Angela	For sure, poor schmuck.

The women now ignore him again and their attention returns to one another. Aldo is still chewing and looking at the group, but his body is otherwise quite lifeless.

Julie	By the way, did you guys give me back my bag of make-up removers?
Veronica	Yeah, in your bag.
Beth	So . . . now do we get to talk 'dirty'?
Sarah	Sure . . . what are you thinking?
Beth	You first.

Sarah	Okay. I am into this VR named Heat.
Gayle	*(alarmed)* Virtual reality?
Veronica	Oh come on, girl – get with it. *(to Sarah)* So . . . ? Go on.
Sarah	Well, he's cool. His body is gorgeous and his voice just goes into me and he knows every part of my body and it is so . . .
Veronica	Less expensive!

All the women laugh except for Julie, who is becoming increasingly attentive to Aldo.

Sarah	Yeah. He's cool. My Mac can materialise him anywhere. In the living room, in the kitchen – man, I can even get him to do the washing up – and of course in my booty room . . . *(general laughter, then Sarah becomes serious)* You know, I miss my real man. But . . . a woman's gotta do what a woman's gotta do!
Gayle	*(looking down)* They're all gone, aren't they? I don't mean the remains. Lots of remains. Walking about here and there. Or just sitting . . . *(points to Aldo)*

The group suddenly stops as they see that Julie is moving across the room to Aldo. She helps him to his feet, straightens his shirt, tie and coat, stroking his body with her hands in a loving and affectionate way. She looks deeply into his eyes.

Julie	So. You. What are you doing here?
Aldo	I don't know really. I think I'm here for a meeting.
Julie	Not surprising, is it? *(puts her hand up to his neck and removes an imaginary piece of lint)*
Aldo	It's not surprising?
Julie	No – a man like you.
Aldo	A man like me?

23

Julie	Of course, a man like you.
Aldo	A . . . man . . . like . . . me?
Julie	*(intensely erotic, almost whispering into Aldo's face, as if they are alone)* A man, a real man, like you. It's not surprising, is it darling, for a man like you to be here?
Aldo	I'm . . .
Julie	You're the MAN.
Aldo	Yes, I'm the man.
Julie	Yes, you're the MAN.
Aldo	I was first.
Julie	You. You. You are always the first.
Aldo	I'm . . . I'm never late.
Julie	I'm sure you're never late, baby. I'm sure you're first and I'm sure you can stay the distance. I'm sure you're always right on time.
Aldo	Thanks.

Julie suddenly breaks off, puzzled by why Aldo said 'thanks'. It is as though the spell has been broken.

| Julie | Don't mention it. |

Julie returns to her chair and sits down to talk to the group, leaving Aldo standing next to his chair, as if called to some form of attention by his own sexuality. He then approaches Julie, kneeling in front of her.

| Aldo | Mum? |

Julie will now divide her attention between talking to Aldo and the other members of the group. What goes on between Julie and Aldo is like a play within a play. It is soft, quiet, affectionate, and seen by the others, but known to them as part of the very thing they are discussing. They take note of it, not troubled by it as such, and are intent on discussing the problems posed by Julie and their discussion.

Julie	Hi baby.
Aldo	Mum?
Julie	Come to Mummy, baby.

She opens her arms gently and he rests his head on her chest. She caresses his head. He wraps his arms softly around her and they become one.

Beth	Should we be doing this?
Gayle	What?
Beth	I mean, we're with a man. We don't know what to do now, do we?
Veronica	I wouldn't call him a man, exactly.
Sarah	Not a real man.
Gayle	But none of us is a mother and he's calling for Mum.
Angela	Look. Who's watching? We have to try to remember what to do with something . . . like him.
Sarah	I think we're better off . . . you know . . . alone.
Beth	It's a lot more fun.
Sarah	We can talk freely.
Beth	Can't do that with a man present.
Gayle	But he doesn't look like a man.

All the women look at Aldo and there is a long pause.

Aldo	Mum?
Julie	Yes, baby.
Aldo	I need you.
Julie	I know you do, baby.
Aldo	I need you, Mum.

Julie	I know, love.
Aldo	Mum, I'm hurting.
Julie	What's the problem, baby?
Aldo	I don't know. Something isn't working.
Julie	Come closer to Mummy, love. *(opens her blouse and puts his cheek to her breast)* Snuggle up to Mum.
Beth	Well . . . what do we do?
Gayle	In what respect?
Veronica	This is a wider problem. We can't solve it on an individual level, can we?
Beth	Yes. After the Catastrophe, what could we do?
Julie	The Catastrophe.
Beth	Exactly, the Catastrophe . . . People have lost everything.
Gayle	Something about the . . . the soul. They . . . who said it, do you remember?
Beth	It was that famous cleric who announced it, the one who was head of state. He seemed to sum it up after the Catastrophe, when he said the soul of man is gone. He was right. All of us knew it. We all knew it. Didn't we? So, we can't blame The Organisation for trying to come up with something.
Julie	It cashed in on it.
Beth	It cashed in on it, yes, of course, but nothing else would work unless it was for profit.
Julie	Loss of the soul, cashed in for profit?
Aldo	Mum.
Julie	Yes, love?
Aldo	I'm in pain.

Julie	Where, baby?
Aldo	All over.
Julie	All over?
Aldo	Everywhere.
Julie	Here.

She offers him her breast. Aldo struggles a bit to get his mouth onto the nipple and Julie spends a few moments helping him settle in. Then he suckles, with the occasional 'mmmm' sound. The group is silent for about a minute as Aldo feeds. They do not appear alarmed; they glance occasionally at the breast-feeding, but otherwise they continue to look at the objects they have in their bags, sorting things out.

Julie	Beth, be a darling and hand me the cloth.

Beth reaches into her bag and brings out a cloth, which Julie places under Aldo's chin, as though to protect her clothing if he spills her milk.

Beth	He is a darling, isn't he?
Angela	A sweetie.
Veronica	Terribly dear.
Gayle	Poor thing.
Angela	Yes, poor darling.
Beth	Whoever does he belong to?
Gayle	Could be anyone, couldn't it?
Veronica	After the Catastrophe, there are so many . . .
Sarah	The men are so damaged.
Beth	We all are.
Sarah	The men more so. They thought they knew what they were doing. They were in charge. Then the Catastrophe, all the rhetoric, all the men trying out their wars and all

that. And then no more answers, and the men stopped talking.

Veronica   And functioning.

Julie   Yes, and functioning.

Beth   Look, Julie . . .

Julie   It's okay. You guys go ahead. I'll catch up with you later.

The other women carefully pack up their belongings and, casting sad but affectionate glances at Julie and Aldo, tiptoe out of the room. Aldo seems to have gone to sleep, but wakes up at the sound of the door being closed.

Aldo   Mum?

Julie   Here.

Aldo   *(slowly moving from the position of suckling, he sits up next to Julie, rubbing his eyes)* I don't know what to do any more.

Julie   I know.

Aldo   I don't even know if I know who I am any more.

Julie   Um.

Aldo   I seem to have lost myself. *(pauses)* To have lost my self.

Julie   I know.

Aldo   I think I knew who I was yesterday, but it seems to have gone overnight.

Julie   It can happen like that.

Aldo   Can it?

Julie   It's not uncommon.

Aldo   Well, it's taken me by surprise. It's been a terrible shock.

Julie   I know.

Aldo	I didn't have breakfast this morning. I forgot, I think. But I got to work.
Julie	That's good.
Aldo	Yes, but then I was supposed to be here for the meeting, but I lost my briefcase, with all my papers, and I don't even know now, for sure, if I had the right date and the right time. I looked at the papers some time ago, but I was in a bad state of mind and I'm just not sure what . . .
Julie	Try not to worry.
Aldo	Yes, I must try not to worry. *(pauses)* I worry a lot.
Julie	I know.
Aldo	I worry about everything, including worrying about worrying.
Julie	I can see that.
Aldo	I spend so much of my time alone.
Julie	Mm.
Aldo	I have no one to talk to, really. No one that I can recall. There may be someone, but I just don't know for sure any more.
Julie	That's hard.
Aldo	I don't know what to do, what actions to take, to . . . to . . .
Julie	. . . to make things better?
Aldo	Yes, to make things better. I don't know what to do.
Julie	Do you want to come to Mummy again?
Aldo	*(looking at her with trembling lips and leaning towards her, but fighting it off)* I . . .
Julie	You're . . .

Aldo	I . . . I'm trying to make it on my own.
Julie	Yes, of course you are.
Aldo	I think I should try to make it on my own.
Julie	Yes.
Aldo	I'm not sure, though.
Julie	I know.
Aldo	I'm not sure that I will make it on my own. I don't even remember why I was supposed to . . . to . . .
Julie	Make it on your own?
Aldo	Yeah, that's it, to make it on my own. I don't know why. It . . . I know that . . .
Julie	People think you should?
Aldo	Yes, people think you should. I don't know if I . . . if I . . .
Julie	Really thought this for yourself?
Aldo	Yeah. I don't know if I believed I should make it on my own. *(pauses)* Mum.
Julie	Yes?
Aldo	Mum, I don't think I ever had the ability to do this.
Julie	To make it on your own?
Aldo	Yeah. To make it on my own. I don't think it was ever in me. I have tried, I think. I know I've worked. I have had a job. I know that I have done things. I can buy tickets.
Julie	Tickets?
Aldo	Yeah, I can buy bus tickets. I know how to cope with public transport. So that's . . . that's . . .
Julie	Something?

Aldo	Yeah, that's something. I mean, that's living independently. Well. I don't know. Maybe. But I don't know how one knows if one is making it on one's own. You see, that's a problem.
Julie	Yes, I see the problem.
Aldo	How do you know? I don't know how you test this. I think I must have been doing it. But I don't know who I am. How can I know if I'm making it on my own, if I don't know who I am?
Julie	It's hard, isn't it.
Aldo	Yes, it's very hard. Very very hard. I . . . Uh . . .
Julie	Something wrong?
Aldo	Have you got a mirror?
Julie	I think so. Let me see.

She leans over, pulls her handbag towards her, and takes out an unusually large mirror, which she opens up. As she does this, Aldo talks.

Aldo	I think it would help if I saw myself. If I could look at myself. I've been alone in this room for a very long time, and I've been starved and very confused, and I think it would help . . .
Julie	To see yourself?
Aldo	Yes, to see myself.

Julie hands him the mirror. Aldo stares at his reflection impassively.

Julie	What do you see?
Aldo	I can't see anything yet.
Julie	Let Mum have a look. *(pauses, then beams, voice raised)* WELL! I see a handsome young man. A handsome young man.
Aldo	You do?

Julie	I certainly do.
Aldo	Can I see?
Julie	Of course. Have a look!

Aldo brings the mirror back in front of him and studies it very quickly, then passes it back to Julie, without speaking.

Julie	Well?
Aldo	We see different things.
Julie	Of course we do. We are different people. But what did you see?
Aldo	The same old thing.
Julie	What is that?
Aldo	I'm gone.
Julie	You're gone?
Aldo	I'm gone, Mum. *(regresses again, falling against her body)*
Julie	*(looking into the mirror)* No, I think you have been away but you are coming back. I see you've had a terrible, terrible day, but you are coming back. Look at the top of your head, just look at your nice black hair. See how strong and thick and ready it is?

Aldo takes the mirror, looks again and puts his hand up to his head.

| Julie | Go ahead, tug. |

Aldo tugs his hair gently.

Julie	What do you think of that head of hair, eh?
Aldo	Seems okay.
Julie	Okay? Okay? It's great. *(takes the mirror off him with enthusiasm)* Now, look at your lovely nose, how forthright and present and pushing itself into the world it looks. Look at your beautiful nose. *(hands him back the mirror)*

Aldo looks at his nose in the mirror and then feels it. Julie reaches over and gives his nose a tug.

Julie   What do you THINK of that nose?

Aldo   Seems okay.

Julie   Okay? Only okay? It's a great nose. And what's that?

Julie takes the mirror and looks into it while talking to him. As she asks about the parts of his face, Aldo responds while looking straight ahead rather blankly.

Aldo   That's my ear.

Julie   Which one?

Aldo   My left ear.

Julie   And?

Aldo   Seems, uh . . .

Julie   *(like a mother talking to a latency-age child)* Now, don't you say 'okay'.

Aldo   Seems great.

Julie   Again.

Aldo   *(elevates a bit)* Seems great!

Julie   And what is that?

Aldo   That's my forehead.

Julie   And?

Aldo   I think that's great, too.

Julie   And what is this?

Julie is now clearly looking at herself, getting rather lost in the mirror, forgetting about Aldo. In turn, he drifts away from her, mumbling and yawning and starting to recline, before gradually falling into sleep as he speaks.

Aldo   My mouth.

Julie   And that's great, too.

Aldo   Yes, Mum.

Julie   And that.

Aldo   My eyes.

Julie   And?

Aldo   Great, too.

Julie   So Mum's baby is . . . ?

Aldo   Great.

Aldo is now fully asleep. Julie gently slips away and out of the door as the lights fade.

Act three

Aldo is sitting in one of the chairs. The mirror is on the arm of the chair, closed, with Aldo's hand on top of it. He is staring patiently, just waiting. He is tranquil and not distressed. He stares at the audience for much of the time, but also looks around, as if he is not familiar with the room and is just having a first look. His serenity is broken by the sound of male voices coming towards the door. Two men in suits enter, with black briefcases, looking self-important.

First Man   *(looking at Aldo)* Ah, very good. You are on time.

Aldo   It's 4.30?

Second Man *(quickly glancing at his watch)* 4.31 now.

Aldo   Ah.

First Man   So you know why we're here, I'm sure.

Aldo   For a meeting?

First Man   That's correct.

Second Man To meet with you.

First Man   To see how things are going.

Second Man Yes, to make sure things are running smoothly.

First Man   So, we have a few questions. I'll start us off, and my colleague will just take a few notes.

The two men sit down on the settee, and both open up their briefcases. The First Man takes out a large ring-bound file, in which certain sections are flagged with coloured paper. The Second Man takes out a notebook and pen.

First Man   So, let's see what we have here. *(pauses to open the first flagged page)* Yes, I can see our office has done some of the work for us – very good, very good – so, to start the ball rolling, tell us very briefly: *(speaks slowly)* how focused do you think you are?

Aldo   Focused?

First Man   Yes, focused.

Aldo   Focused on . . . uh . . . on . . . does it say on what?

First Man   *(a bit thrown)* Well, I don't know exactly. Just a minute.

The Second Man has been writing down the proceedings, but now halts in mid-sentence, raises his pen and looks with some slight doubt at his colleague.

Well, that's a good question. It doesn't say. How about we leave it that your answer to this question is to, ah . . . *(momentarily lost, but then beaming and looking at his colleague)* FOCUS on the question! And when you did, when you focused on it, you got a result. So, let's move on now to the second question.

Aldo sits up a bit, somewhat taken in by the fact that he seems to be doing rather well, even though he has no idea what this is about.

How well do you think you delegate?

Aldo   Delegate?

First Man   Yes, how well do you think you delegate?

Aldo   Could you say to whom?

First Man   To whom?

Aldo   Yes, could you say to whom I was to delegate?

First Man *(perplexed, looking at his book)* Okay, let's see. Delegation . . . delegation . . . delegation . . . Just looking here, just reading it through a bit. No, it doesn't say who you are delegating to. Just seems to be asking how well you delegate.

Aldo Maybe it's incomplete.

First Man Incomplete?

Aldo Maybe the question isn't finished.

First Man That's a possibility, isn't it? That's possible.

The Second Man stops taking notes, raises his pen, and appears slightly annoyed with his colleague for interrupting his work.

I wonder what we can do.

Aldo Maybe you could take the question back and they could . . . um . . . they could finish it. It's hard to answer a question like that.

First Man *(looking at his colleague)* Did you get that?

Second Man Yes.

First Man What did you write down?

Second Man 'Maybe you could take the question back and they could finish it.'

First Man That's what I thought I heard. *(Aldo shrinks in his seat, fearing the worst)* Do you REALISE *(Aldo now curls up, nearly foetal)* how BRILLIANT – how absolutely brilliant – this reply is? Do you have any idea? *(looking at his colleague)* Do you think he has any idea how important this moment is?

Second Man I've no idea. Let's see.

First Man *(turning back to Aldo)* Well, I asked you how well you delegated, and you said you couldn't answer the question and that I would have to go back and get more details. You have just DELEGATED me! *(beaming)*

Second Man *(now also beaming)* I think this is a first.

First Man   An absolute first.

Second Man Do you think there's any point in going on after that?

First Man   *(laughing like a nervous but excited schoolboy)* Well, I don't
             know, I don't know. Who knows what could come next?

Second Man That's right, who knows what could come next?

First Man   It's tempting just to continue.

Second Man Let's go for it.

*During this exchange, Aldo has reassembled his body, moving back to a
sitting position, and has a glazed grin on his face.*

First Man   Okay, let's see. The next question . . . right . . . What
             scope do you have for flexibility?

Aldo   For flexibility?

First Man   Yes, flexibility. But before you ask me about flexibility in
             relation to what – no more focus and delegation here. This
             time I can give you more info. What scope do you have
             for flexibility IN DEVELOPING NEW SKILLS?

*The First Man is very pleased that he has been able to add something
which seems challenging and assured. The Second Man nods and writes
very quickly.*

Aldo   Could you say what new skills?

First Man   What new skills? Well . . . *(now thrown again, looking back
             to the file)* Um . . . let's see. What new skills? Skills . . .
             skills . . . skills . . . Let me see what it says. It says after
             that: 'and do these skills increase target and performance
             standards?' Let's see – is your answer 'what new skills'? Can
             we take that as your answer?

Aldo   My answer?

First Man   Yes, I can't see how . . . I think . . . well . . . In answer to the question about flexibility, you have asked about what, but I don't know quite what we can do. So, would you mind if I just wrote down that you answered with a question. Is that okay with you?

Aldo   Well, can't you say that if we had more details we could probably answer this question. I mean . . .

First Man   You mean if we were MORE FLEXIBLE! *(beaming)*

Second Man   My God!

Both men get up, high-five one another and start to close up their briefcases.

First Man   It's incredible.

Second Man   I know.

First Man   I've never seen anything like it.

Second Man   Nor will we again.

First Man   Nor will we again.

Second Man   Will anyone believe this?

First Man   You've got it all down?

Second Man   All down, word for word.

First Man   Fantastic.

Second Man   We should go.

First Man   Yes, absolutely. They may think we've been enjoying this too much.

Second Man   Yes, they might say that we should have stopped after the first question, that we knew then what we had here.

The two men get up and walk towards the door.

First Man   Yes, they might, but we must not worry.

They leave without any acknowledgement of Aldo, who is left in the empty room, staring at the closed door, then looking at his hands, as if something has been taken from him but he doesn't know quite what. Then the door bursts open again and the First Man pops his head in.

First Man   Oh – in all the excitement, forgot to say – please stay put, don't move, someone will be with you soon.

Aldo has opened his mouth to speak, but the First Man leaves again before he can do so.

Aldo   I . . . I'm not sure. Have I been to the meeting? What do you think? I don't know what to think. I think it was a meeting, but I'm not sure it was THE meeting. *(pauses)* Well, they seemed pleased, anyway. I . . .

There is a knock at the door.

    Yes?

Voice   May I come in?

Aldo   Um . . . Who are you?

Voice   I'm the Director. You don't have to open the door. I've heard from my colleagues and know your responses, and I wanted to meet you for myself and perhaps ask a few more questions.

Aldo   Why did you knock?

Voice   Why did I knock?

Aldo   Yes, everyone else just walks in, but you knocked.

Voice   That's because I have to.

Aldo   You have to?

Voice   You'll see for yourself if you open the door.

Aldo   I'll see why you have to knock?

Voice   Yes, you will see quite clearly.

Aldo	I don't know. I'm suddenly afraid.
Voice	I don't think you have anything to be afraid of.
Aldo	But I am.
Voice	I understand.
Aldo	I don't know what I'm going to see.
Voice	I understand.
Aldo	Seeing you must be upsetting.
Voice	I understand why you think that.
Aldo	There must be something different about you.
Voice	Different?
Aldo	You knocked. You have to have my permission to see me. And when I see you I will know why you had to knock. It makes me think . . . well . . .
Voice	Think?
Aldo	I don't know. I don't know what to think. I can't actually think. I don't know what to say, what to do, what to think.
Voice	I've upset you.
Aldo	Yes, terribly. I . . . It's probably not your fault. This has been a very bad day for me. I didn't have anything to eat, almost all day. I've been starving.
Voice	Anything else?
Aldo	Else?
Voice	Is there anything else wrong?
Aldo	Um . . . *(struggling)* Well, there have been, I mean, there are of course all sorts of things that go wrong, or have been wrong, or don't seem to work out.

Voice   Your sexuality, for example?

Aldo   My sexuality?

Voice   Your sexuality leaves you thinking that you've got things wrong?

Aldo   My sexuality is . . . well . . . is . . . it's . . . it's just that sexuality itself is, you know, just kind of . . .

Voice   Weird?

Aldo   Yes, weird.

Voice   I understand.

Aldo   You do?

Voice   Perfectly.

Aldo   You understand perfectly.

Voice   Why don't you open the door?

Aldo walks slowly but surely towards the door, extends his arm at full length, opens the door and recoils several feet. At first we see a bright – almost blinding – light flowing; then the Voice enters. He is wearing a sort of papal gown, large and flowing, but yellow rather than white and with some quirky additions: some fashionable scarves and a gaudy ring on his finger.

             Don't be alarmed.

Aldo   *(falling back into his chair)* Who are you?

Voice   That's a good question. It is often asked of me. It's not so easy to answer.

The Voice beckons flowingly to Aldo to bring him a chair, which Aldo does in a sort of trance. The Voice then sits down as if on a throne, as Aldo retreats to his chair.

             My colleagues were very impressed with your answers. Over the moon, really. And in such circumstances I am called to visit the subject – which is our way of referring to you, Aldo – just to visit and to have a brief chat about things.

Aldo   *(meekly)* A chat?

Voice   Yes, just a chat.

Aldo   You mean, idle talk?

Voice   Yes, exactly. That's exactly right, Aldo. It's really the only way one can talk about it.

Aldo   About 'it'?

Voice   About sexuality, remember?

Aldo   Oh yes . . . *(slowly recollecting)* Yes, I remember.

Voice   It's why you let me enter.

Aldo   Why I let you enter?

Voice   Yes. Your sexuality is a bit haywire?

Aldo   Haywire?

Voice   A bit off?

Aldo   It's off. Yes, it's off. I can't seem to . . .

Voice   . . . think it?

Aldo   Yes, it, I find it . . .

Voice   . . . revolting?

Aldo   Yes, it's . . .

Voice   . . . disgusting?

Aldo   Yes, it's so . . .

Voice   . . . filthy?

Aldo   and . . .

Voice   . . . obscene?

Aldo   Yes, and I don't know what to do . . .

Voice   . . . with . . . ?

Aldo   . . . with my . . .

Voice   . . . penis?

Aldo   Yes, I don't know what to do with it . . .

Voice   . . . beyond . . . ?

Aldo   . . . peeing?

Voice   Yes, beyond peeing.

Aldo   Yes, I don't know . . .

Voice   . . . beyond playing with it?

Aldo   P-p-p-p-playing with it?

Voice   Beyond wanking?

Aldo   *(somewhat flustered and frightened)* I don't know where this is going. I mean . . .

Voice   You don't like talking about your sexuality?

Aldo   No, I don't see the point.

Voice   You don't see the point of understanding why you feel obscene, filthy and disgusting?

Aldo   Do I?

Voice   You've just said so.

Aldo   I think I was just answering questions.

Voice   Your answers have taken you to your sexuality and to your depravity.

Aldo   To my depravity?

Voice   To your fantasy.

Aldo	My fantasy?
Voice	You know, the fantasy where you suck a blue tit's anus while you're being penetrated from behind by a small white horse.
Aldo	What? How do you . . .
Voice	. . . know about that?
Aldo	What do you . . . ?
Voice	. . . plan to do with it?
Aldo	What does this . . . ?
Voice	. . . mean about you?
Aldo	A blue tit?
Voice	A coal tit, actually.
Aldo	And . . . ?
Voice	You're holding it in your left hand, its small body trembling with fear, and you push your mouth up under its tail, and as you begin to gently suck its anus you see a white horse.
Aldo	White?
Voice	A WHITE horse.
Aldo	How small?
Voice	About three feet high and four feet long, with a long white tail and soft furry ears.
Aldo	And it is . . .
Voice	It has a beautiful white erection and it pushes its penis into your anus as you are . . .
Aldo	. . . sucking the anus of a coal tit?
Voice	YES!

The Voice has become increasingly aroused and as he shouts 'YES!' there is a kind of shudder to his body. Aldo is rapt but terrified. There is a pause as the Voice forgets Aldo for a moment. Then he begins to gather himself together and rises from his chair.

> YES. YES . . . Well, that was very good. I'm pleased to have met you and to see, as my colleagues have said, how impressive you really are. I don't think I have any further questions. Let's see . . . *(looks at his large gold watch)* It's almost time for the meeting to close. I think this is the end, but it's 4.49, so why don't you wait until the very end before leaving. It could be that others will want to meet with you.

Aldo   Others?

Voice   Well, I'm probably last on, I think. But you never know. Best to stay till the end.

Aldo   And when is that?

Voice   You don't know?

Aldo   Well, I've lost my briefcase and my watch is broken.

Voice   Poor boy, you really are at a loss, aren't you?

Aldo   Yes, well, I am rather.

Voice   Yes, indeed. Poor boy. Rather at a loss. Well, I'm sorry, I can't help you with this. I've got to be on my way. There's a woman in Room 567 whom I may have to question.

Aldo   Room 567?

Voice   Yes, you've not been there yet, have you?

Aldo   No, just here, in 228.

Voice   Ah, well, 567 is very special. Another time, then. Who knows, we may meet again. Bye.

The Voice exits. Aldo looks at his hands, then his feet. After half a minute he stops and stares out at the audience as the lights go out.

.

Act four

Aldo is sitting on the floor, legs crossed, looking around, waiting. He hears someone coming and quickly looks toward the door. A man enters, dressed as a courier, wearing a brown uniform with a brown cap. He is carrying a parcel and a duffle bag. Aldo jumps to attention.

Courier   Mr Hurt?

Aldo   What?

Courier   Mr Aldo Hurt?

Aldo   Who are you?

Courier   You don't recognise me?

Aldo   You?

Courier   No, not me.

Aldo   Who are you, if you aren't you?

Courier   *(beaming and enjoying what he takes to be something of a joke)* I'm from BS.

Aldo   BS?

Courier   Brown Service! You've surely seen our vans all over the place. We're famous.

Aldo   Oh, yes. Of course.

Courier   You've been away?

Aldo	Away?
Courier	I'd guessed you've been away if you didn't recognise BS when you saw it.
Aldo	No, I haven't been away. I've been here . . . quite a long time.
Courier	In old 228?
Aldo	You know this room?
Courier	Of course, I deliver in this room quite frequently.
Aldo	'In' this room?
Courier	What?
Aldo	You said you delivered 'in' this room.
Courier	Oh, yes. That's jargon for 'delivering a package'.
Aldo	I see.
Courier	You have some kind of identification on you, do you?
Aldo	Well, no actually. I . . . *(looks around)* I've lost my briefcase. I don't think . . .
Courier	What about a wallet?
Aldo	Oh, of course. *(reaches into his back pocket, then stands up and searches all the pockets in his trousers and his coat)* I don't know . . . I don't seem to have my wallet on me.
Courier	You don't have your wallet on you? How could that be?
Aldo	I don't know, really. It's been a very bad day.
Courier	Have you been mugged?
Aldo	I don't think so. But it has that kind of feeling.
Courier	What does?
Aldo	The day. The day has the kind of feeling like I've been

mugged, or that I've lost something. I don't know, it's hard to say.

Courier   Well, I'm in a difficult position.

Aldo   You are?

Courier   Very.

Aldo   What's your problem?

Courier   Well, I've got to deliver this to a man called Aldo Hurt and you have no identification on you, so I can't give this to you. Unless you have some way of proving you are Aldo Hurt.

Aldo   I don't see how I could prove it.

Courier   I'd have thought there must be a way.

The Courier pauses to think for a long time.

I have an idea! I'm going to reel off some names, at great speed, and when you hear your name called out, then you repeat it. Do you get it?

Aldo   Well . . . yes.

Courier   Ready?

Aldo   I suppose so.

The Courier opens up a notebook full of other BS customer names and, while walking around, reads them off at considerable speed.

Courier   Roger Francis, Gary Naples, Frank Dart, Sylvan Mestor, Harry Tower, Tom Dickster, Dick Homburg, Harry Heart, Harry Nation, Nat Osborne, Frank Fester, Oberline Gaston, Berry Lineker, Gentle Francis, Alton Fowler, Nalton Restler, Shirty Alton, Alton Tower, Henry Altoburg, Lars Hurtenstein, Altuna Hurtzberg, Altona Hasberg, Hurtberg Altonitis, Altona Ture, Turrie Alto, Alto Hearst, Hurt Alton, *(Aldo nearly raises his hand at this last name, but quickly stops himself)* Talton Alto, Alto Nurt,

> Nurt Alto, Ventor Bender, Nick Brand, Brank Fosswonder, Alto Notnurt, Hurt Alto, Alto Alto, Aldo Hurt, Alto Hurt, Alton Firstberg, Hurt Aldo . . . *(the Courier slows down, wording the names almost as if in slow motion)* Alton Hurting. Hurt Are. Hurt Aldo. *(pauses)* Are you Hurt Aldo?

Aldo   Yes I am.

Courier   I don't know if that's true.

Aldo   It is.

Courier   If it is, then I'm afraid BS cannot deliver this to you.

Aldo   But I am hurt.

Courier   But you are not Hurt Aldo, you are Aldo Hurt.

Aldo   I am both.

Courier   That's impossible.

Aldo   No, it's true.

Courier   You cannot be two people at the same time.

Aldo   I'm not.

Courier   You just said you were.

Aldo   No, I didn't.

Courier   Then what did you say?

Aldo   I can't remember, but it wasn't that.

Courier   BS cannot deliver to you.

Aldo   What's in it?

Courier   I don't know.

Aldo   Then how do you know you can't deliver it to me?

Courier   This has nothing to do with what it is – it's about who you are.

Aldo	I would have thought it has everything to do with what it is and nothing to do with who I am.
Courier	What do you mean?
Aldo	I would have thought that what's in the package is very important. Why else are you here, delivering it to Room 228? *(Aldo gains strength through his speech)* You are BS, and BS doesn't deliver just any old thing, only BS stuff, which has to be important. It doesn't matter who I am, it matters what BS has.
Courier	That's a strange way to put it.
Aldo	These are strange times.
Courier	I have an idea.
Aldo	You do?
Courier	Yes. You don't know who you are.
Aldo	Well, I do.
Courier	No – sorry – but you don't. I called out your name and you didn't respond, so I have to conclude that you are not who you think you are. In fact, you think you are Hurt Aldo rather than Aldo Hurt, so actually you are the reverse of the person to whom I am meant to deliver this package. You are him backwards.
Aldo	That sounds about right.
Courier	What does?
Aldo	I am backwards. Things are backwards. I expect I may well be Hurt Aldo. It sounds more accurate.
Courier	So, you admit that you are not Aldo Hurt?
Aldo	It no longer sounds right.
Courier	But if you are in fact Aldo Hurt, and I had reason to think you were . . . You can't just change your name like that.

Aldo	But it feels more correct.
Courier	But it's not for you to change your name. It's not yours to change. It was given to you by your parents. It's on your birth certificate. It's on your social security certificate. The state knows you by that name. Only actors can change their names.
Aldo	But you changed my name.
Courier	Me?
Aldo	Yes, I remember it now. You said to me, very carefully, 'Are you Hurt Aldo?', and as I was hurt, I said yes. You identified me. And I think you linked me to my proper name.
Courier	That's intriguing, but it doesn't get us out of our problem.
Aldo	Which is . . . ?
Courier	I cannot give a package addressed to Aldo Hurt to Hurt Aldo. That would be against the rules. But I had an idea a moment ago, and it might work.
Aldo	Um . . . ?
Courier	If you were to join BS then we could inspect the contents of this package together.
Aldo	Join BS?
Courier	Yes! If you joined, if you worked for us, then I could deliver this package to you . . . well . . . we could open it.
Aldo	How would that be possible?
Courier	It's easy, actually. In fact *(he reaches into the duffle bag)* we're always looking for recruits. I have a BS uniform which you can slip into, and a simple form – all you have to do is sign your name and you're part of BS.
Aldo	You want me to change my clothes?

Courier	That makes it official.
Aldo	But what about my other job?
Courier	What other job?
Aldo	The job I must have had before joining BS.
Courier	Well, I don't know about that. Anyway, lots of people have two or more jobs. So, what's it to be: do you want to slip into BS or not? What have you got to lose?
Aldo	I could change my mind afterwards?
Courier	Well, you could quit, I suppose.

Aldo takes off his suit, down to his underwear, and slips into the BS costume. While he does this, the Courier, humming to himself, opens up a book with a form inside it and fills out some details, before rummaging about for other odds and ends. He hands the form and pen to Aldo, who signs his name.

Aldo	How do I look?
Courier	Like a newborn!
Aldo	A member of BS?
Courier	Absolutely! Now . . . let's get down to business. Here's a package for Aldo Hurt, so let's open it up and see what's in it.

They open up the package to find a letter, which they both simultaneously read out loud.

Both	'Dear Aldo Hurt. Thank you for attending the Meeting. You have met our criteria and at next year's review, you will be interviewed in Room 235, which, as you will appreciate, is a step in the right direction. Please find enclosed a cheque for £12.50 to cover your expenses for the day. Hoping you have a good and productive year, we remain, as ever, your colleagues. P.S. You are now free to leave the room.'

There is a long pause, neither person knowing what to say next.

Courier Well, that's clear enough.

Aldo What is Room 235?

Courier Well, I can tell Hurt Aldo this, of course, though I could not have told Aldo Hurt, but 235 is the room where BS delivers its half-life reports.

Aldo Half-life?

Courier Yes, a special room, where we let the person know how he or she is doing, having already had, statistically, their half-life. It's an important moment.

Aldo But I'm in my thirties, I think.

Courier Yes, but it's not to do with age. Half-life has to do with radiation. It's a metaphor really, of just how much time – work-wise, or professionally – one has left. You get there by virtue of what in the trade is called 'radiation potential'. You seem to have quite a high radiation level.

Aldo What is that?

Courier Well, it's sort of like charisma, but not quite. It's an emanation. Something that you have been emitting. *(pauses)* Well, look, it's really time for me to push off. You too.

Aldo Yes.

Courier Ready then?

Aldo What about my clothing?

Courier Well, bring along the suit. You can always use that. We have really good BS parties, if you decide to stay with us.

They leave the room. Aldo has left his plum-coloured scarf behind, draped on a chair. A minute passes and then all the characters who have appeared in the play – except Aldo – walk slowly back into the room, chatting, putting their hands on one another's shoulders. Those in uniform have loosened their ties or taken certain bits off, indicating that what had been worn was part of some form of costume.

Julie   Wow! I never thought he would make it.

First Man   I know. Well, do we think he really did?

Courier   Well, he left the room.

Several   Yes, he left the room.
together

Veronica   Do you think that THERAPLAY worked for him?

Voice   Well, he certainly went through all the paces. We informed him he had a meeting to attend, without telling him with whom or for what. We removed the contents of his refrigerator so that he had nothing there for breakfast. And we arranged for the drains man to come during his lunch hour, so he was starving by the time he got here.

Julie   And we broke his watch and stole his briefcase, so he was deprived of a sense of time and purpose. He became desperate when he was isolated.

Second Man And we saw what happened when he was with you girls. That was a real . . .

Julie   It was a real regression, no doubt.

Courier   I mean, you WERE his mother. He was reborn right there and then. When THERAPLAY works, it really works. Just think – we have one day, just one day with a target, and we have to deconstruct them and put them back together. I mean, this shit really works!

Julie   Yeah, who'd have thought it? *(pauses)* And he passed reprofessionalisation, thanks to you guys. It was great, you guys were great.

First Man   Thanks, Julie.
and Second
Man

First Man	You were a true pro yourself.
Julie	Thanks, it was . . . well . . . it was something. And then he even passed resexualisation.
Voice	Only just, and I nearly fucked it up.
Courier	How did you come up with that blue tit thing?
Voice	I heard about this guy in the sixties who was trying to get out of the draft. He said he was afraid of going off to war because he didn't think there were any blue tits in Vietnam, and his sanity depended on having one within arm's reach at all times. They asked why and so he told them.
Julie	And?
Voice	He got off.
First Man	Yeah well, good for him.
Gayle	And we have to thank Hank!
Veronica	Oh absolutely – brilliant direction.
Voice	Well, he is incredibly experienced, and the fact that he used to be a psychoanalyst certainly helped.
Second Man	Yes, poor old psychoanalysis. But then until THERAPLAY came along, who could presume to turn an entire life around in one day?
Voice	*(contemplative)* You know, all along this made sense: it was an accident waiting to happen. *(they all laugh)* No, I mean it. Rather like psychoanalysis itself was, for a while, a step in the right direction. But it took Alexander Fistright-Rathburst – with his breakthrough theory of anthropology – and his wife . . .
Sarah	Leonora.
Voice	. . . And his wife Leonora – a good actress, though not a great one – to marry these two professions. If you study a

person long enough, if you do the research – and Marge spent . . . how many weeks on this guy?

Sarah   I think it was two months.

Voice   Okay, two months – shadowing him, sending various expert observers into his life, having folks phoning him up to put him through false questionnaires. It took two months but then we had this guy's private anthropology down to a T. And then all we had to do was take Hank's direction and put Aldo through his transformational paces.

Julie   Well, we did our job. Do you think . . .

Voice   That it worked? Well I do, but who knows? That's not our issue. We're just actors, it's a play. We have to leave the rest of it to the real experts.

In different ways, they all voice their agreement.

Julie   Okay everyone, let's clear out.

They all leave the room noisily, embracing each other and patting each other on the back. The room is silent for a minute or so. Then the door slowly opens and Aldo re-enters, closing the door behind him. He is dressed oddly. His clothing is a mélange of the various costumes worn by the other cast members: a bit of a suit, something from the BS outfit, a part of the papal gown, and so on.

Aldo   *(addresses the scarf on the chair)* Ah, there you are! You must have thought I'd left you. Left you all behind, all by yourself. That wasn't nice of me, was it? It wasn't nice of Daddy to leave you all to yourself, just lonely, and left.

He puts the scarf to his face and smells it. He senses that it has been held by others. He holds it out in front of him and smells it again.

What's this? What's this? Where have you been? Who else has been here? You smell, you smell FOUL . . . absolutely foul. Like some kind of perfumery with so many scents it adds up to a bum. How could you smell like bum! *(he brings it slowly back to his nose and sniffs again)* Wait. Wait.

I can . . . I can recall something nice . . . I can smell it. It's in there . . . in amongst all that bum, all that poo. What is it? *(pauses for a long time)* Mum? Is that you, Mum . . . me? Is that my Mum-me, my lovely Mum . . . me? *(falls to his knees)*

The play slows right down now: a breakdown in slow motion. There are long pauses between Aldo's statements and questions. When he looks at different members of the audience, he gazes directly into their eyes.

I thought . . . I thought . . . I'd done so well. I seemed to have pleased so many people. I had a good report. I was so hungry and starved, and at a loss. I've lost my name, but I thought I was on the road to recovery. Everyone has contributed so much. I've been helped. But can I go on? Can I go on? I don't seem to have . . . I just don't seem to have what the others have. *(now looking directly at individual audience members, moving from one person to the next)* I don't think I have what YOU have, or what YOU have, or YOU OVER THERE. I don't know how you do it. I can't seem to keep myself together. So much work . . . I'm so much work. Don't you think so? And YOU, how do YOU manage? And YOU, where do you go for help? I think I'm finished. I thought I would have to wait until I died, but I'm done. I have no idea how to make ends meet. I don't know where I'm meant to go, or who I'm meant to be, or anything like that. *(there is the sound of a slow hand-clap off-stage by one person, then joined by others, getting louder and louder)* Oh, God. I'm sorry. I'm sorry to have gone on like this. In front of so many of you. I'm so sorry. Please forgive me. I'm going now. Not to worry. Not to worry.

Aldo walks backwards, bowing to the audience. He bumps into the door, opens it with his left hand, and quickly disappears, leaving the door ajar.

Curtain.

Old Friends

A play in one act

Cast

Harry Nastorp

Serge Kavorsky

Gerald

Jacqueline

Old Friends

The scene is an institutional sitting area, like a meeting room in a corporate office. There is a small table with a coffee machine to stage left, with several sofas and a few chairs stacked against the wall. The room is without windows. Harry Nastorp – a man in his mid-forties wearing a crumpled light suit – sits in one large sofa. He glances through magazines, waiting, obviously unable to read and quite ill at ease. Harry is shy, vulnerable, and uncertain of himself. He looks nervously at his watch several times before the door opens and Serge Kavorsky enters. Serge is also in his forties, but is taller than Harry. He is dressed in an elegant suit and carries a briefcase. Serge is commanding and full of confidence, but exudes a cold, menacing attitude, somewhat like Vladimir Putin. He nods briefly at Harry and sits down opposite him, in a similar chair, partly facing the audience.

Serge   *(icily, glaring at Harry)* I really don't know what I'm doing here.

Harry   *(his voice and mannerisms are a bit like Woody Allen's)* I think we have to talk about it.

Serge   There's no point.

Harry   *(emotional, confused)* No point?

Serge   No point. It's over.

Harry   How can it be over?

Serge   It just is. It's dead.

Harry   After so many years, you're just saying it's over?

Serge   I'm not saying it, I'm reporting it.

Harry	Reporting it?
Serge	Yes, it is an observation.
Harry	Whose observation?
Serge	It's obvious. I'm simply reporting the obvious.
Harry	*(gains some strength through objection)* Nothing is obvious.
Serge	It's really very simple.
Harry	How can it be simple? I was awake all night thinking about it.
Serge	Well, that's your problem. I slept soundly.

Serge smiles in a contemptuous and triumphant way, putting his hands above his head and cracking his knuckles.

Harry	How can that be?
Serge	Because there's no conflict. I have accepted it. *(adopts an attitude of indifference)*
Harry	But we've known each other for, what . . . ?
Serge	What difference does that make?
Harry	What difference does twenty years of friendship make?
Serge	It's past. Over. *(looks around the room, bored)*
Harry	But it must have meant something. *(pauses)* I mean, it must mean something. *(pauses again and looks at Serge in expectation of a reply)* You, or we, can't just throw that away, surely.
Serge	It's not for us to throw it away – it was already gone. It died long ago.
Harry	Why didn't you say something?
Serge	I did.
Harry	*(startled)* When?

Serge	Two years ago, at the opera.
Harry	What opera?
Serge	War and Peace.
Harry	What happened?

Serge changes his attitude at this point, leaning forward in his chair and pointing his finger at Harry as he speaks.

Serge	I asked you what was the matter.
Harry	And?
Serge	And you said 'nothing'.
Harry	I said 'nothing'.
Serge	Your EXACT words.
Harry	Well, maybe nothing was wrong.
Serge	*(loudly and angrily)* It was wrong all right, and you lied.
Harry	How did I know what you were talking about?
Serge	*(almost yelling, but still very controlled)* That was clear to both of us.
Harry	Serge, I can't even remember that moment.
Serge	*(quietens down, his voice now resigned)* Because I was beneath your contempt.

The characters achieve a sort of parity through the following argument. It is almost childlike and reveals a glimpse of former times when this might have been pleasurable.

Harry	You think I was beneath your contempt?
Serge	No, I said that I was beneath YOUR contempt.
Harry	Why was I beneath your contempt?
Serge	I said that I was beneath your contempt.

Harry	No, you weren't.
Serge	How would you know?
Harry	Because it would have been my contempt you were beneath and I have no memory of your being beneath it.
Serge	I should know.
Harry	Why?
Serge	Because I was beneath it.
Harry	How do you know?
Serge	*(again in a fury and speaking slowly)* Because I SAW it.
Harry	*(as if truly interested in what Serge saw)* What did you see?
Serge	An expression on your face.
Harry	An expression?
Serge	An expression.
Harry	What expression?
Serge	You smiled.
Harry	I smiled? I smiled? What's wrong with smiling?
Serge	It was the smile of contempt.
Harry	Well, show me, what does that look like?

Serge raises his eyebrows and smirks.

Serge	There, like that.
Harry	But that was just an idiotic look on your face.
Serge	It was how you looked.
Harry	Like an idiot?
Serge	Like someone full of contempt.

Harry	And you've ended our friendship of twenty years because one night at the opera I had an idiotic look on my face when you asked me if anything was wrong?
Serge	You knew perfectly well what I was asking and you knew exactly the answer you were giving, both in word and in gesture. You might just as well have said 'fuck off'.
Harry	'Fuck off' to your question, what was the matter?
Serge	Your face and your words said 'fuck off'.
Harry	But why would I react like that to such a question?
Serge	That would have been for you to answer, but now this is moot.
Harry	Moot because you say the relationship is over with?
Serge	I am only reporting the obvious.
Harry	But we have families. *(gestures around the room as if others are present)*
Serge	So what?
Harry	We can't do this to our families!
Serge	*(absolutely indifferent)* Why not?
Harry	Because they know each other so well. They're friends. We hang out together.
Serge	That's not my problem. They'll get over it.
Harry	This is like a death sentence.
Serge	*(enjoying himself)* More like an execution, Harry. Yes, more like an execution.
Harry	So . . . why do it?
Serge	I didn't – you did.
Harry	You mean, at the opera?

Serge   That was after the execution. I have no idea when you
           actually killed us off.

*The mood shifts at this point. Although Serge remains a cold and dominant
figure, it seems that he is now recollecting a painful truth. Harry's innocence
is somewhat disingenuous. His voice sounds thinner and he has a hard time
looking at Serge.*

Harry   *(feebly attempting to gain the high ground, dwelling on the
           word 'I')* When I killed us off? I haven't killed us off.

Serge   You deny that things are different?

Harry   Things?

Serge   Our ostensible 'relationship'.

Harry   *(looks at Serge, suddenly less the histrionic innocent)* Well, I
           HAVE been upset with you.

Serge   *(furiously indignant)* UPSET?

Harry   Yes. *(pauses, looks at the floor)* You can be too aggressive,
           too hard sometimes.

Serge   WHAT are you talking about?

Harry   I don't want to get into this.

Serge   WHY NOT?

Harry   Because it will seem small-minded.

Serge   Well, you are small-minded. You might as well own up
           to it.

Harry   *(frightened by Serge's force of personality)* What do you
           mean? It's . . . it's . . . not going to help us if . . . if . . . you
           take a hostile position like that.

Serge   *(icily)* We aren't going to be helped.

Harry   So you say.

A mobile phone rings. Both Harry and Serge quickly search their pockets and Harry answers his phone.

(in a raised voice) Hello? *(to Serge)* It's Monica. Hello, darling. Well . . . I'm, in fact I'm just talking to Serge. No, we're not having lunch, we're . . . we're actually having a meeting. Talking . . . talking business. I . . . no . . . I don't think that's a good idea. No reason, no reason . . . okay . . . *(looking bewildered, he hands the phone to Serge)* Monica just wants to say hello.

Serge puts his hands up as if to say no, then reaches for the phone reluctantly.

Serge   *(perfunctory, but not hostile)* Hello, Monica. Thanks, that's kind of you. Well, I began the project about two years ago and, yes, I am glad it's finished. No. Nothing in particular. *(looking at Harry)* We sound strange? No, there's nothing . . . well, Harry will tell you later. It's nothing dire. No. Nothing to worry about. But we need to get back to . . . that's okay. Yes. Bye. Yes, I will. *(Serge hangs up and throws the phone back to Harry)*

Harry   *(yelling, hurt)* You threw the phone!

Serge   I didn't want to take it in the first place!

Harry   You didn't have to take it.

Serge   I had no choice.

Harry   No choice?

Serge   I had no choice. You handed it to me before I could think.

Harry   *(calmly, as though now gaining the upper hand)* Before you could think. Well. I suppose that's rather crippling for you, isn't it, since your thinking seems to be guided only by revenge. Revenge for some smile I gave you at War and Peace.

Serge	You've just acknowledged that by then you didn't like me any more.
Harry	I acknowledged what?
Serge	That you didn't like me. You said I am competitive.
Harry	You were . . . you are. *(pauses)* But anyone who knows you or chooses to be your friend has to accept that about you . . . Anyway, I don't want to get into it.
Serge	We are into it.
Harry	Well, we are into it. If we talk about it, can we sort it out then?
Serge	No.
Harry	Then why talk?
Serge	That's my point.
Harry	What's your point?
Serge	There's no point in talking. It was your idea to meet.
Harry	So why did you agree?
Serge	To make an official end to it.
Harry	An OFFICIAL end?
Serge	Yes, official.
Harry	So, this is an official meeting?
Serge	In a manner of speaking.
Harry	So, just what is an 'official meeting', then, even as a manner of speaking?
Serge	It's the announcement of a decision.
Harry	Not of a conversation.
Serge	Exactly. This is . . .

Harry   Your 'policy'?

Serge   Well, I'm glad that you at last seem to understand.

Harry   I don't understand any of this.

Serge   You're just being coy.

Harry   Coy?

Serge   Yes. You love your innocence. You never know anything. It's always left up to others to tell you about what you yourself have done. Look at you – all wide-eyed, wounded innocence.

Harry   I am innocent. I don't know what has driven you to this point.

A mobile phone rings, and again both characters search for their phones, in a great rush. Serge answers.

Serge   *(affectionate but impatient)* Yes? Yes. I'm talking to him right now. Yes. Yes. Yes. Yes, I've told him.

It becomes clear to Harry that Greta and Serge have discussed this meeting and have come to some form of decision. Harry is stunned and frightened, as if confronted with a form of reality that is impossible to believe.

Harry   Is that Greta?

Serge   Yes.

Harry   What are you talking about?

Serge   *(to Greta)* No. I don't think that's a good idea.

Harry   What isn't a good idea?

Serge   *(to Greta)* No. I think it's enough to do this. There's no need.

Harry   No need for what?

Serge   *(to Greta)* Look, let's talk about this later. I'll be home in a few minutes – in an hour or less. Yes. Yes. No. No, no, no. Yes. Okay.

Harry	Wait!
Serge	*(to Harry)* What is it?
Harry	I want to talk to Greta.
Serge	What for?
Harry	I just want to talk to her.
Serge	What for?
Harry	I don't know, I just think I should be able to talk to her.
Serge	*(to Greta)* Harry wants to speak to you. No. Yes. No. I don't think so. Are you sure you want to? Okay. *(to Harry)* She will speak to you.

Serge places the phone on the table between them. Harry pauses and stares at it, then looks up at Serge and reaches for the phone with trembling hands. He speaks in a fragile, broken voice. The conversation has many pauses and Harry raises his voice when he realises he cannot understand what Greta is saying.

Harry	Hello, Greta. I, uh, is . . . all is well? Sorry? I'm sorry, I didn't quite hear that. You what? I, what? I'm a flirt? Oh, sorry, I'm hurt? You're hurt? What happened? Sorry, it's hard to hear. You are hurt? *(to Serge)* She's hurt herself?
Serge	Jesus Christ. Keep talking.
Harry	Greta, you are hurt? What? I . . . I . . . hurt you? I did . . . ? When? The other night? Where? At Ben's Grill? What did I do . . . ? I what? I didn't what? I didn't say goodbye? Greta, that's not true. Um. Um. Yes. Yes. Um.
Serge	What's all the umming?
Harry	*(to Serge)* Just a minute, please. *(to Greta)* Um. Um. Yes. Yes. No. No. That's . . . not what happened. No. No. Please, Greta. That is not what happened.
Serge	What happened?

Harry	*(to Serge)* Wait, Serge. *(to Greta)* Greta, that is not what happened. No. No! When I dropped the fork on the floor I promise you I did not put it on your serviette. No.
Serge	Yes you did.
Harry	*(to Serge)* What?
Serge	You did. You . . .
Harry	*(to Serge)* Just a minute, Serge, you're both speaking at the same time. *(to Greta)* I did not. I really don't think so. But . . . Okay . . . Well, if you insist that I did then it was entirely unconscious and I must apologise. No. I apologise. I certainly did not intend to put a soiled fork on your serviette. And, no, I did not refuse to say goodbye. *(Harry and Serge stare at one another fiercely as Harry continues talking to Greta)* What? What smile . . . ? What do you mean, 'that smile'?
Serge	You know what she's talking about.
Harry	*(still looking at Serge but speaking into the phone)* What?
Serge	You know what she's talking about. It's that same smile.
Harry	*(to Serge)* Just a minute. I can't talk to both at once. *(looks away from Serge and up at the ceiling as he talks into the phone)* Greta, what smile? What do you mean, 'content'? Did you say 'content' or 'contempt'? Are you sure? The smile of content?
Serge	No, contempt.
Harry	*(to Serge)* No, Serge. Greta is saying 'the smile of content'.
Serge	That's not possible.
Harry	*(to Serge)* Do you want to talk . . . *(to Greta)* Greta, I . . . What do you mean by 'the smile of content'? The smiling cheese? What smiling cheese? I don't know what . . . The cat that got the smiling cheese? I think it's, do you mean the Cheshire Cat? Is that what you mean? No, not

73

Cheshire Cheese, it's a cat from Cheshire that is smiling because it got the milk. I . . . OKAY. *(to Serge)* She wants to talk to you.

Harry hands the phone back to Serge.

Serge	*(to Greta)* Yes. No. No. It was NOT content, it was CONTEMPT. His smile is one of contempt. That's not what I said. I did not say that it was the smile of content. I never said that. I always think very clearly about everything I say.
Harry	Wait a minute – you two have been talking about this?
Serge	*(to Greta, ignoring Harry)* Look, no. Look. Think about it. The difference is clear. A smile of content is a smile for when one is pleased with oneself, while a smile of contempt is where one's pleasure is at the expense of the other who is deemed to be beneath one. Yes. Yes. Yes, that's right. It was a smile of contempt. No. I don't know. Cheshire is a cheese, yes. I don't know. How should I know? He's very fucked up.
Harry	Who's fucked up?
Serge	*(still ignoring Harry)* Yes. Don't worry. No. No. I won't tell him.
Harry	Can I speak to her?
Serge	*(to Greta)* Yes, don't. No. There's no need to do that, this is enough.
Harry	Do what? Can I please speak to Greta?
Serge	*(to Greta, roaring with laughter)* No. We can't. Okay.
Harry	*(yelling hysterically)* Greta! Greta! Greta! Please speak to me!

Serge recoils with a look of horror and discomfort on his face, and throws the phone to Harry.

Greta . . . Greta? Greta? *(looks at the phone)* She hung up.

Serge	Of course.
Harry	Why?
Serge	Why not?
Harry	Because . . . because . . .
Serge	Because why?
Harry	Because we're friends.
Serge	No, we're not. We're no longer friends. It's over.
Harry	But not with Greta.
Serge	OH YES, VERY MUCH SO WITH GRETA.
Harry	This was a joint decision?
Serge	I don't have to answer that.
Harry	You do.
Serge	It's none of your business.
Harry	It certainly is my business. Our friendship is part of my life. I have a right to protest.
Serge	Protest all you like. No one is listening.
Harry	What does that mean?
Serge	It means you fall on deaf ears.
Harry	I can't believe you said that.
Serge	What difference does it make? You don't believe in what anyone says, no matter how it's put.
Harry	No matter how?
Serge	Poetry is wasted on you. You hear nothing.
Harry	I thought you said YOU heard nothing.
Serge	What?

Harry	You said you heard nothing, now you say I hear nothing.
Serge	I did not say that.
Harry	Did not say what?
Serge	What you just said I said.
Harry	What part of what I just said you said did you not say?
Serge	Something about deaf.
Harry	Exactly. It's you that's deaf, not me.
Serge	I'm deaf?
Harry	You've just asserted it.
Serge	I'VE asserted that I'M deaf? *(laughs)*
Harry	Well, you may laugh, but I have a memory.
Serge	Oh? A memory? What do you remember?
Harry	What did you mean just then when you told Greta that you didn't think something was a good idea?
Serge	What are you talking about?
Harry	You and Greta. You told her on the phone that you didn't think there was any need to do whatever it was that you were thinking of doing.
Serge	I have no idea what you are talking about.
Harry	No idea?
Serge	If I did, anyway, it's none of your business.
Harry	None of my business – that you and Greta are thinking of doing something to me and so my future is somehow hanging at your disposal?
Serge	Would that it were.
Harry	What?

Serge	What is the point of all this?
Harry	The point is becoming clear, isn't it?
Serge	Clear?
Harry	*(stronger now, as if rallying himself to deal with something more serious)* Yes, it's becoming clear. Clearly you intend me some kind of harm.
Serge	Don't be ridiculous.
Harry	I know what I heard.
Serge	You know nothing.
Harry	I know what I HEARD.
Serge	Which is to know nothing. Nothing will come of nothing . . . *(laughs to himself)*
Harry	That's the intent, obviously.
Serge	*(confused)* What do you mean, that's the intent?
Harry	To turn me into a no-thing.
Serge	Don't be so dramatic.
Harry	Me, dramatic? You quoted Lear, not me.
Serge	Because you are Lear.
Harry	You just said that. There's no thinking behind such a comment.
Serge	Try me.
Harry	So, how am I Lear, then?
Serge	Because you're interested only in false flattery and you're blinded by your pride. You don't know a friend, even when you have one.
Harry	All this because of a smile?

Serge   Your smile was just a signifier.

Harry   Such a small thing.

Serge   Small gestures always carry more significance than large ones.

Harry   If you are Othello.

Serge   This is meant to be, what, a pregnant comment?

Harry   Have it delivered, then.

Serge   Why? To indulge your wish that this endlessly idiotic conversation should continue?

Harry   You would execute me again? Killed once, I cannot be terminated again.

Serge   *(childishly)* Melodramatic wanker!

Harry   You're the wanker.

Serge   You are.

Harry   No, you are.

Serge   You just spank the monkey. *(roars with laughter)*

The door opens and Gerald rushes in. He is a man of similar age to Harry and Serge, and is also wearing a suit. He is obviously pleased to see them.

Gerald   Hey! What you guys up to? *(he is met with silence)* Ooooo . . . I say. Arrived at the wrong moment, have I?

Gerald realises something is wrong but cannot adjust to it. Serge is removed and icy; Harry is eloquent and furious. Instead of sitting down, Gerald walks over to the coffee machine and pours himself a cup, then stands there rather paralysed.

Serge   No, probably the right moment.

Gerald   *(with false bravado, as he is unsure what is going on)* Ah! Well, then. I just thought . . .

Harry	What?
Gerald	Well, it looked as if I'd spoiled all the fun. I could hear Serge's infectious laugh and just popped in to see if it was him and damn, there he is – in the flesh! *(moves very slowly back towards the door)*
Harry	Don't be deceived.
Gerald	*(stops in his tracks and looks frightened)* Deceived?
Harry	By the notion that he is in the flesh. I rather think he is possessed. Something has taken him over.
Gerald	Oh dear . . . *(looks hesitantly back and forth, then slowly sits in a chair)*
Serge	Don't worry, Gerald. No need to worry.
Gerald	But I heard laughter.
Serge	We were talking about masturbation.
Gerald	*(relieved and looking bright again)* Oh good! Fantastic. Great subject. I mean, I suppose it is a hoot, isn't it? The forbidden topic. Did you know that the Americans don't allow references to, what do they call it . . .
Serge	Pleasuring yourself.
Gerald	*(laughs)* Yes, that's it – great phrase! Did you know that they've just passed legislation in some of the States that forbids references to wanking. Isn't that amazing?

There is an uncomfortable silence. Gerald looks back and forth at Serge and Harry.

Harry	Serge called me a wanker.
Gerald	Of course he did.
Harry	Of course he did?

Gerald	He . . . *(looking confused)* Well, of course we call one another that – we say it all the time. So he called you a wanker.
Harry	He meant it!
Gerald	He MEANT it? He . . . meant what?

Serge makes a coughing sound to indicate that he is present. Gerald laughs anxiously.

	Oh, of course . . . what did you mean, Serge? Why is Harry a wanker?
Serge	Because he is a jack-off; a spumacide.
Gerald and Harry	SPUMACIDE??
Serge	A spumacide.
Gerald	*(delighted)* That's hilarious! I've never heard that before. *(noticing Harry looking devastated, he tempers his enthusiasm)* What is . . . a spumacide?
Serge	It's suicide by wanking.
Harry	Gerald . . . *(pauses for an ostentatiously 'dramatic' effect)* Serge has taken to saying things which he THINKS are clever but which have no thought behind them. He just . . . well, ironically, he just ejaculates: he is an EJACULATOR.

Gerald now gets up, leaving his coffee on the table. He opens his arms as if to ask what on earth is going on.

Gerald	Spumacide? Ejaculator? Hey! Guys. Guys! What's up?
Serge	It's all about Lear and Othello. It's nothing. We're almost finished.
Gerald	Lear and Othello . . . What are you talking about them for? I mean, they're trouble, aren't they? *(he is met with*

silence) Well. I really do seem to have walked into something.

Harry · You'll find out about it soon enough, anyway.

Gerald · *(walking to the door)* About what?

Serge · You'll find out about Lear and Othello soon enough.

Gerald · And wanking?

Harry · You see, Gerald, Serge is trying to have you believe that 'Lear' and 'Othello' are code words for some project we're working on, something . . .

Gerald · To do with wanking?

Harry · To do with turning something into nothing.

Serge · To do with nothing that comes from nothing.

Harry · To do with nothing that seeks to create nothing.

Gerald · Here? In the workplace?

Harry · Between people.

Serge · It's nothing to do with me.

Gerald · To do with Harry, then?

Serge · It's Harry's thing.

Harry is holding his head in his hands and seems to have collapsed.

Gerald · *(very uncomfortable)* Look, Harry. Have you been caught spanking, here in the office? Is this about wanking in the workplace?

Harry · *(slow and tired)* No, Gerald, this is not about wanking in the workplace. This is about Serge ending our friendship. He has turned executioner and declared that we are over. That is what this is all about.

Gerald · And Othello and Lear?

Harry   He quoted Lear's 'nothing will come of nothing', and from there I thought of Othello – making something out of nothing.

Gerald   Othello made something out of nothing?

Harry   You know, the scarf . . . I mean the handkerchief.

Gerald   Ah, yes, the one that Iago planted and . . .

Harry   Yes, yes. Anyway, Serge saw a smile. And Greta may be Iago.

Serge   Ha! That's just perfect. Just perfect. Full of conspiracy theories because he cannot accept any responsibility for what he's done.

The door opens and another colleague, Jacqueline, enters the room. She is in her mid-thirties, quite smartly dressed, and although professional, she has a hearty sense of humour. Her entrance gives Gerald the chance he has been waiting for and he makes a dash for the open door.

Gerald   Well . . . got to go! Good luck with the production.

Gerald exits, closing the door.

Jacqueline   Production?

Serge   It's Gerald's idea of what's going on in this room.

Jacqueline   You fellows are producing something?

Harry   Serge is, not me.

Jacqueline   Not a CO-production? *(wiggles her hips in a brief simulation of intercourse, before heading to the coffee machine)*

Serge   *(icily)* Actually, it is.

Jacqueline stops dead in her tracks and stares at the two men.

Harry   No, it is not.

Serge · · · You're as much a part of it as I am. You're more a part of it than I am.

Jacqueline · · · *(confused, but trying to be bright)* Well, Harry, it looks like Serge is trying to give you credit for something you more than deserve, but you won't take it. I mean, why look a gift horse in the mouth? *(seemingly released by what she has said, she proceeds to the coffee machine)* Boys, boys, BOYS.

Harry and Serge · · · Boys?

Jacqueline · · · Um? *(turns as she pours her coffee)*

Serge · · · *(disapprovingly)* You said 'boys'.

Harry · · · Yes, boys! *(approvingly)* You called us 'boys'. And I think you're right.

Jacqueline · · · *(surprised)* Oh . . . I don't know. Did I say that? Well, I suppose I meant that . . . you know . . . boys will be boys.

Serge · · · I want to know what you mean by that.

Jacqueline · · · I'm not sure I know.

Serge · · · Then why throw it around, if you don't know!

Harry · · · Serge, look . . . she's . . .

Serge · · · Shut the fuck up, Peter Pan.

Jacqueline leaves her coffee on the machine and tiptoes slowly towards the door.

Jacqueline · · · I . . . I didn't mean to cause any trouble. I guess I've just been in a strange mood today. I suppose if boys can be boys, then girls can be girls?

Serge · · · Or an idiot an idiot – never mind the gender.

Harry · · · That is totally uncalled-for.

Serge · · · I didn't call for anything. I simply make observations.

Jacqueline   *(stops and stares at Serge)* I don't know what's the matter with you, Serge. I think you're . . . you seem . . .

Serge   I'm not interested in your impressions, Jacqueline. If you have something to say, then say it.

Harry   Jacqueline, this is nothing to do with you. Please don't worry about it. We're having a confrontation. I think it's best if you . . . you know . . .

Jacqueline   *(still staring in real fear at Serge)* Yes. Leave. I . . . of course. But . . . but nothing awful is going to happen here, is it – is it?

Harry   No. Of course not.

Serge   There are no promises. Who could ever promise you that nothing awful is going to happen? Only God – the Almighty Himself – knows how to call the future. For all we know, someone could be killed in this room.

Jacqueline   *(terrified)* Oh my God!

Serge   That's right: oh my God. He would know. I personally have no idea what's happening in this room now, or what will happen in the next five minutes, or the next five years. This room and the events that take place in it are not part of my brief.

Harry   *(looking at Jacqueline)* He's very clever, Jacqueline. He can pretend not to be here and to have nothing to do with – as he puts it – the 'events that take place' in this room, but I assure you he is here, as we can see, and his manner is . . . well . . . is . . .

Jacqueline   *(moving quickly to the door)* I must go. I'm sorry.

Jacqueline exits. There is a long silence as Harry and Serge engage in a choreography of glancing at one another and then looking away. Then Serge looks at his watch.

Harry   A time problem?

Serge	No, not at all.
Harry	You were looking at your watch.
Serge	No, I was observing my watch.
Harry	And what was your observation?
Serge	That I must leave in five minutes.
Harry	Five minutes?
Serge	Actually, seven minutes, to be exact.
Harry	Why seven minutes?
Serge	Why not?
Harry	Seven minutes to what?
Serge	To the end.
Harry	The end?
Serge	The end.
Harry	Serge, look at me. *(Serge looks formally, briefly, then averts his gaze)* You're looking away.
Serge	I obliged you. I looked at you.
Harry	What did you see?
Serge	That's my business.
Harry	Serge, what did you see?
Serge	Someone.
Harry	You saw me!
Serge	I did?
Harry	Yes!
Serge	I'm not so sure.
Harry	I tell you, it's me you saw.

Serge   And what is that?

Harry   What . . . what?

Serge   Who then, Harry, who is that?

Harry   Someone who is being executed.

Serge   No, Harry, someone who doesn't care . . .

Harry   About?

Serge   Someone who cares nothing about being a friend. You
            disappeared. You simply left, and you leave it to me to
            announce the end of it all.

Harry   Well.

Serge   Well what?

Harry   There is some truth in what you say.

Serge looks at his watch and picks up his briefcase.

            Why are you looking at your watch? Why are you
            gathering your belongings?

Serge   I have to go.

Harry   Go? Why?

Serge   I've called a car.

Harry   Can't you ask the car to wait?

Serge   Why?

Harry   Because, Serge, if not, fate will prevail.

Serge   Fate?

Harry   Yes.

Serge   So what?

Harry   You don't even know what I mean.

Serge	Oh yes I do.
Harry	You know what it means if fate prevails?
Serge	Yes.
Harry	Okay, tell me.
Serge	It means that . . . Look. I'm not going there. It was your idea to meet like this. I said we had one hour. We have *(looking feverishly at his watch)* five minutes left, then I leave.
Harry	Your cab is our fate?
Serge	Sentimental rubbish. You ended this, but you're assuming no responsibility.

A phone rings again. Serge puts his briefcase down, both men search their outfits, and Serge answers. His voice changes dramatically: he sounds charming and light-hearted.

	Oh, Thierry! Yes. I'm fine. No. No problem. In an hour, yes, that's good. And Greta is ready. So . . . yes. Right. Talk to you later. *(hangs up)*
Harry	Thierry?
Serge	It's none of your business.
Harry	Our Thierry? Thierry, our boss, our Director?
Serge	Whatever.
Harry	Thierry, to whom I introduced you eight years ago, after you'd begged me for ten years to find some way to bring you together? *(pauses)* Was it my imagination that you asked if I would give you his address? Was it my imagination that you asked Monica and me if we were sure it wasn't a problem that you invited Thierry and his wife to stay with you?
Serge	It's not my problem that you were, and are, small-minded.

Harry	Small-minded?
Serge	Unbelievably so. *(looks at his watch)*
Harry	That's right – look at your watch. Watch time going past. We're all fucked, aren't we, Serge? Sooner, much sooner rather than later, we're all screwed by time. So, between then and now, between our beginning and our end, what is there?
Serge	You're full of shit.
Harry	I'm full of protest! I'm full of fury. I'm full of your executional mentality.
Serge	You're simply a display. *(both men pause)*
Harry	*(calmly yet icily)* Why did you agree to this meeting?
Serge	Ah!
Harry	There is a reason, isn't there? *(Serge smiles)* You didn't come to talk, did you?
Serge	Of course not.
Harry	You've just come with announcements.
Serge	Pretty close.

There is silence for a few moments. Harry is now worried and distracted, while Serge fixes him with a more authoritative gaze.

Harry	You've got something else to say, haven't you?
Serge	Yes.
Harry	What is it?
Serge	*(looking at his watch)* In a minute.
Harry	In a minute? What in a minute?
Serge	In a minute I will tell you what I have to say.
Harry	All along?

Serge   All along?

Harry   All along you've had something to say?

Serge   What's the difference?

Harry   I thought you were here because I asked you to come.

Serge   That's your narcissism, isn't it, Harry?

Harry   I thought it was friendship.

Serge   Clearly that was never true between us.

Harry   Clearly?

Serge   I have no idea who you are.

Harry   Of course not.

Serge   *(taken aback)* Of course?

Harry   You have no idea who I am because the you who is thinking right now is some – what do the shrinks call it? – some weird split-off part of your personality, like the Nazi doctors who were nice guys at home but turned into vicious bastards when they went to work.

Serge   I don't need to answer that.

Harry   You can't. Just as you can't allow our friendship – all the times we dined together, the holidays we took together, the conferences we attended, the football games we went to, the way our kids played and grew up together, the . . . You can't let yourself think that now, can you, Serge? Because that would just blow this fascistic part of you out of the water, wouldn't it? Or are you so efficient at killing nowadays that you can kill off the barbecues in the garden, the trip to Malta, the time your mother stayed with us because your son had measles, the time we climbed to the top of . . .

Serge   *(interrupting)* That's enough! I don't want to hear any of this.

Harry	No, of course not. Because to hear is to remember, and to remember is to be recalled to these moments, and you can't bear it because if you let yourself feel these memories then your fascist self would dissolve.
Serge	You flatter yourself, Harry, to think for one moment, even one nanosecond, that this analogy holds. I've not ended the relationship. It died. And it died because you disappeared and left Greta and me with the remains. For years we wondered why you no longer saw us.
Harry	That's not true – I did see you.
Serge	Oh yes, nominally. But you dropped us. We went from the first league to the fourth division. You dropped us and we didn't know why, and we were hurt.
Harry	I'm sorry.
Serge	I'm not interested in your sorrow.
Harry	Yes, but what you say is right.
Serge	What difference does that make?
Harry	Because we should talk about this.
Serge	There's no point.
Harry	That was my fear.
Serge	What?
Harry	That you would say there was no point in talking.
Serge	It's too late.
Harry	No, Serge, you can't bear frank talk. If I'd said to you years ago that I found you and Greta too ambitious – to the point of walking over good friends to climb a ladder – then you would have ended the friendship just as you are now. You can never bear to talk things through, and I had no choice but to step back from the intensity of our relationship. I don't excuse myself, but I'm telling you this is why.

Serge   You're baiting me. You're trying to bait me.

Harry   Into what?

Serge   Into asking you what you mean about social climbing.

Harry   You don't need me to tell you what I mean – you know.

Serge   This is such bullshit. You are so small-minded.

Harry   Oh yeah? Well, let me give you just one example. One small example. That will please you, won't it, because being so small, it will seem to prove your point. Do you remember when you pleaded with me to find some way for you to visit my accounts in Japan? And I set things up for you. Arranged for you to visit my accounts, to be the guest of people in four different cities, and then one year later I passed by your house and Akira was walking out your front door.

Serge   So?

Harry   Akira was my main contact in Japan. My main contact. And you and Greta had invited him to come and stay in your house and you never told me. I had to find out by accident.

Serge   What is the point you're making?

Harry   The point? The point is that you ripped off my main account in Japan. My point is that in climbing the ladder you'll walk over anyone. Akira was the first step to your ascension in Japan.

Serge   Akira was just a nice guy. I liked him and he liked me. You're telling me that you can intermediate in the development of my friendships! Who do you think you are, some kind of God?

Harry   He was my main contact, and you ripped him off. You didn't even tell me in the months before he arrived that he

91

and his family were going to stay with you. Why, Serge? Why not tell me?

Serge   I would have.

Harry   Would have?

Serge   Of course.

Harry   When?

Serge   Soon enough.

Harry   SOON enough? Are you joking? What do you mean, soon enough? It was too late. You never told me.

Serge   I would have told you, but I had a lot on my mind. You're making a mountain out of a molehill.

Harry   No. This is one example of what you might call my small-mindedness, but in this one episode is the story of your ruthlessness, of the way you use people. You have good sides to you – really great aspects – but this part of you is awful.

Serge   That's enough. I'm not here to listen to your Calvinist preaching. I've had enough of your homoerotic mourning, your pathetic hurt feelings, your insufferable innocence . . . your collection of wounds. Your house is like a hospital, your kitchen like an operating room, your bedrooms like wards for the sick . . . your . . . *(looks at his watch)* Oh shit. Okay. I have something to tell you.

Harry   You mean . . . the reason you came?

Serge   Yes.

Serge pulls out an envelope and extracts a folded letter, which he opens and reads slowly.

This letter is from the Board and is signed by Thierry. He's asked me to read it to you. 'Dear Harry Nastorp, we appreciate the twenty-one years you have given to the firm, but we have no further use for your services. Your desk is to be cleared by the end of the working day, when you are to leave your keys with the Receptionist. Sincerely, Thierry Observa.'

Serge passes the letter to Harry, who reads it for himself. He is stunned. While he reads, Serge collects his briefcase and stands up.

Harry   You've killed me.

Serge   I've delivered a letter.

Harry   You've ended our friendship and turned Thierry against me. You've killed me. There's nothing left for me now.

Serge   You'll find something. You will always find something.

Harry   I . . .

Serge   I don't want to hear it.

Serge leaves the room and slams the door. Harry, holding the letter in his hand, stares very briefly and quizzically at the audience and the lights go out.

Piecemeal

A play in four acts

Cast

Virginia Flount

Charles Flount

Tom Henders

Will Menses

Wanda Menses

Clarissa

Virginia's Understudy

Robert Flount

Prompter

Act one

Scene one

*A large room in an upper-middle-class English flat, which functions as a
sitting and dining room, with a coffee table, comfortable sofa and side
chairs, as well as a dinner table. There is a window stage left, overlooking
the street outside; a door in the stage-left side of the back wall, which
provides access to the kitchen and other parts of the flat; and a passageway
stage right, which leads to the flat's entrance hallway. The dinner table is
stage left, a few feet from the window, and centre stage is the living area.
There is a small writing desk against the wall stage right, with a large
mirror above it.*

*The curtain rises to an empty room, but after a few moments Virginia
Flount enters with a bowl of crisps in her left hand and a hairbrush in her
right hand. She is in her mid-forties, wearing a smart but rather outmoded
dress with a floral pattern. She is attractive but looks rather worn. She
walks about the room with a subtle sense of fatigue, and when she speaks
there is a barely suppressed despair in her voice. But she comes across as a
woman who has always tried to look on the bright side of life.*

*Virginia places the crisps on the coffee table, in the centre of the room,
stands back to look at the arrangement, and then looks around, inspecting
the room in anticipation of guests arriving. By accident she catches sight of
herself in the mirror above the writing desk. She is rather girlishly drawn to
her image, as if the mirror beckons, and she stands in front of it, casually –
almost carelessly – brushing her hair. What begins as an ordinary action
turns into something of an anxious examination as she stops brushing and
comes very close to the mirror. Humming a little tune to herself, she turns*

her face first to the left, then to the right, to look at her profile close-up, before stepping back a few paces and repeating the action, still humming. She then walks back across the room and bumps into one of the chairs around the dinner table. She lets out a slight 'oh!' before walking very slowly back towards the mirror. Halfway across the room, looking into the mirror, she extends her hand and smiles broadly, as if practising a greeting, but then sighs; her shoulders sag and she gives up. She turns round and walks to the window, passing around the dinner table, and looks out for a few moments before she resumes some tidying – fluffing cushions, arranging the flowers.

Virginia   *(calling out in a friendly but anxious tone)* Charles, darling. It's 7.30 and they'll be here any moment. Charles?

Charles   *(off-stage, from the kitchen)* What?

Virginia   I said it's 7.30 and we don't have the appetisers on the table. Charles, where are you?

Charles   What? I can't hear you.

Virginia   *(to herself)* Of course you can't hear me. You never hear me. I mean . . . who does? Who's listening? I can go through the motions, can't I? I've been here a thousand times before – just fluffing and fretting and looking and . . .

Charles bursts into the room. He is a good-looking man, also in his mid-forties, comfortably dressed and embodied, but slightly patronising and falsely confident.

Charles   What were you saying?

Virginia   Oh, who cares.

Charles   Oh, darling . . . *(he moves across the room and gives her a patronising hug)* Of course I . . . we . . . care. We always care.

Virginia   Oh, Charles. *(she is derogatory and he winces)* You care by word. And by deed, love, by deed?

Charles   By deed? What deed?

Charles tries to inject false humour and fails. He bobs about a bit as he tries to assess quite where Virginia is. He is anxious about the party, active yet not productive. He does not quite know what to do with himself, and this vulnerability shows as he continues to engage his wife.

Virginia   Exactly.

Charles   Exactly what?

Virginia   *(enjoying her ascendancy)* Precisely.

Charles   Oh. Oh. All right. What have I done?

Virginia   *(now cheerful and resigned)* Or haven't?

Virginia's change of mood is mildly alarming to Charles, as if she has found amusement at his expense and he does not know how to respond.

Charles   Haven't? Ah! I haven't brought out the olives, the . . . the . . .

Virginia   The salmon, the peanuts, or the champagne.

Virginia returns to the mood of a woman organising the final preparations for her party, and Charles is momentarily relieved and relaxed.

Charles   Yes. Damn. I am awful. Absolutely awful. Aren't I?

Virginia   *(changes mood again and her next comment is violent and out of place)* Oh, fuck you, Charles.

Charles   *(stunned, off-balance, he attempts humour but it is strained)* Fuck me? When? *(approaches Virginia with a false leer, trying to put his hand on her bottom)*

Virginia   *(surprised and angry in a flash)* Oh, fuck off! Don't you dare touch me.

Charles   *(recoils)* Fuck off? *(pauses, looking at her with concern)* Whatever is the matter? *(stands a few feet from Virginia, his hands now dropped to his sides, at a loss)*

Virginia   Oh, what's the use . . .

Charles   *(irritated)* Well, talk about it. What the hell's the matter?

Virginia	Oh, Charles, there's . . . there's just no support.
Charles	I do support you.
Virginia	Yes, I know, in your own way. Of course you do. But . . . you don't understand. Did you see the laundry in the hallway when you came up?
Charles	*(feigning innocence)* Yes.
Virginia	Well, what did you think it was doing there?
Charles	What did I think it was doing there?
Virginia	When you saw the laundry, what did you think?
Charles	Ginny, love, I don't think I thought anything.
Virginia	That's the point.
Charles	I should have thought something?
Virginia	No, of course not, because you're not meant to think about these things. Are you? I mean, there's a load of laundry, of your things, on the stairs, and it wouldn't occur to you that you were meant to take it up to your chest of drawers. It wouldn't occur to you to think about this any more than it would occur to you to think about the fact that we are low on washing-up liquid, or that we are nearly out of stamps, or that the hoover needs repairing. *(slumps onto the sofa)* I don't want to blame you, but you're just not here. Well, not in my world. Or in the world. But who of you are?

Virginia has drawn in on herself, no longer looking at Charles. He still stands in the middle of the room and tries to recuperate matters through his play with her slip of the tongue.

Charles	Who of me are? *(chuckles)*
Virginia	*(to herself)* Well, you laugh.
Charles	I didn't laugh. I'm serious.

Virginia   You can catch me out, but you . . . oh . . . What's the point. Anyway, we have other things to worry about.

Charles   We do?

Virginia   Go on! Get the things. *(jumps up and heads towards the dinner table)*

Charles   Oh shit.

Charles runs out of the room towards the kitchen, as if going to get something, but also in order to flee his wife's sudden bolt into action. Virginia walks around the room in silence for a few moments and then flops back onto the sofa. She starts talking to herself again, but her head is thrown back, and she seems to be trying to regain some position through a kind of reflective power.

Virginia   I should write a bloody column for the . . . the . . . for some paper. Maybe a weekly. 'Letters from home.' No – that's too weak. 'Letters from the front line.' Yes, that's better: 'from the front line'. *(reading the imaginary column out loud)* 'Last night I gave my two hundred and sixty-sixth dinner party married to my current husband, now topping the number of dinner parties for my former husband. It is still twenty-three behind the boyfriend I had during my twenties, whom I served diligently while he went to graduate school, but I nonetheless celebrated this moment in the history of my servitude by putting a pin on my loved one's favourite chair and I waited . . . oh I waited . . . in delicious expectation of the moment . . .'

She breaks off, goes to the small desk and takes out a pin. She laughs, runs over and puts the pin on a side chair next to the sofa. She stands back admiringly, but then retreats from her action as she hears her husband approaching. Charles enters the room.

Charles   Well . . . you have a strange look on your face.

Virginia   Me?

Charles	*(turning round, as if addressing someone behind him)* Yes – of course you.
Virginia	*(a bit thrown)* Charles, whoever are you talking to?
Charles	To you.
Virginia	*(irritated)* Okay, Charles. Very funny. Haw haw. Anyway . . . *(the doorbell rings)* Oh Christ.

Virginia leaves through the passageway stage right where, off-stage, there is the front door to their flat.

Charles	*(to himself)* Don't worry. *(puts out the salmon and other starters)* Just get through this, old man. No problemo. No problemo. *(trying to walk about in an imperial way)* Capisce, baby? Capisce?

Virginia returns to the room, arm in arm with Tom Henders. He is much younger, in his early thirties, and, in coat and tie, is more formally dressed than Charles and Virginia. He is obviously shy and uncomfortable, and does not seem to know how to stand or what to do with his arms or body.

Virginia	So! Look what handsome man I found on the street.
Charles	Who goes there? What rake has taken my·woman?
Tom	*(embarrassed, awkward and depressed)* Hey, hi . . . *(sits on the sofa)*
Virginia	Hard to find your way?
Charles	No, Ginny, Tom knows his way . . .
Tom	No . . .
Virginia	I meant . . .
Charles	He knows . . . *(to Tom)* you've been here . . .
Tom	About two years ago.
Charles	That long?
Virginia	Two years, three months.

Charles	She never forgets a thing.
Tom	Yeah, that's good. *(not sure of the meaning of what he has said)*
Charles	Champagne? *(pouring it as he asks)*
Tom	Oh great. Yeah, good. *(he is unable to make eye contact with either of them)*
Virginia	*(softly, gently, and with sincerity)* Oh Tom, darling.
Charles	*(loudly, without sincerity, in stark contrast to his wife's manner)* We are so sorry.
Tom	*(bracing himself)* Thanks. Yes. I know. It's okay. Well. It's not really. But, you know, it's not so easy.
Charles and Virginia	Of course not.
Tom	But, you know, I just. Well . . . *(looks at Virginia as if asking to be rescued from this acutely uncomfortable situation)*
Virginia	We loved her so much.
Charles	Yes, she was wonderful.
Tom	Yes. Well . . . *(looking down at his hands, folded neatly on his lap)*
Charles	It's deeply disturbing.
Tom	*(fearful of what might now be said)* Sorry?
Charles	It's criminal, the number of women dying of breast cancer. A pandemic. We talk about the loss of life in wars. Well. Look at what's happening under our noses.
Virginia	Charles, I'm sure Tom doesn't . . .
Tom	It's okay.
Charles	I only meant that . . .

Tom	Yeah, I agree. It's a crime.

Embarrassed, not knowing what to do with himself, Charles now sits on the chair with the pin and explodes in pain.

Charles	*(leaping up)* What the – shit! Ow!
Virginia	Oh my God.
Tom	*(shocked)* Charles?
Charles	I'm attacked! *(swirls round as if he does not quite know what has hurt him)*
Virginia	Charles . . . Oh . . . Oh . . . dear . . . that's my drawing pin.
Charles	What the hell is it doing here?
Virginia	I must have lost it.
Charles	Must have lost it?
Virginia	Yes, I guess so.
Charles	Well, it wasn't here fifteen minutes ago when I was reading the Standard. How did it find its way to my chair?
Virginia	*(feigning distraction, fluffing her hair, then offering canapés to Tom)* Oh . . . I'm sure there's some explanation. Some . . .
Charles	Good Christ. My bottom hurts . . . Sorry, Tom. But. Well. Who'd have thought that one of Ginny's drawing pins would find its way onto my chair?

Charles sits down but glares at Virginia. He is clearly enraged but also bewildered by his wife's behaviour. Tom looks back and forth between the two of them, rather suspecting they have been in conflict.

Tom	Well, these are strange days.
Virginia	*(as though talking to herself)* God. They certainly are. *(sits down on the sofa and stares into the middle distance)*
Charles	*(hesitant, but serious)* You think about her a lot?

Tom	All the time. All the time. I see her. I see her, you know.
Virginia	You see her? *(pauses, looks at Charles)* Of course you do.

Tom's demeanour suddenly changes dramatically. He becomes alert and excited. As he speaks, he looks back and forth at Charles and Virginia, examining their faces for signs of response to what he says.

Tom	I mean, I SEE her. In the last few days, walking on the streets. In fact, just fifteen minutes ago, wearing a black leather suit. She never had a black leather suit, and she looked great in it. I know it was her. I could hear her voice. I followed her into a, into a . . . I don't know, it was some kind of council estate, but I lost track of her. That was only just a few minutes ago. I know she's out there somewhere. It . . . I just feel it. It's so strange.

All are silent for a few moments.

Virginia	She was, so . . .
Tom	All my dreams have red in them, too.
Virginia	*(softly)* Well, her red hair was just radiant, like some beacon from God.
Tom	I know. And, her blue eyes . . .
Charles	Like jewels.
Virginia	*(embarrassed by Charles's comparison)* More than that, but it's hard to say . . .
Tom	*(angrily, looking directly at both Charles and Virginia, as if stating a fact that must not be contested)* I hear her voice.
Virginia	Yes, it was so . . .
Charles	Like Marilyn Monroe's . . . *(now Charles seems to be talking to himself, looking up at the ceiling)*
Virginia	. . . sensual and . . . *(looking at Tom, anxious about his sudden change of behaviour)*

Tom It was childlike, child working class. It . . . she was working class. And I saw her just now, walking on the estate. She glanced back at me, as if she wanted me to follow her. What should I do? Should I run after her and yell her name?

Charles *(his mood has changed and he is businesslike)* Er, Tom, how did you meet? I mean, in the first place.

Tom Oh. Well . . . *(rather overwhelmed by the prospect of telling the story)*

Virginia Maybe not now, Tom. It's just so recent.

Tom Three weeks.

Charles Good God.

Virginia *(irritated)* What?

Charles I meant, good God, that's just so recent, so raw. So . . .

Tom *(sarcastically and in clear irritation with Charles's false discourse)* It's death, Charles. It sucks.

Charles It sucks, yes, it sucks. *(nodding his head, looking acutely uncomfortable)*

Tom *(as if in physical pain)* Oh God.

Charles and Virginia What?

Tom I forgot the wine.

Virginia Oh, for heaven's sake, forget it, it's okay.

Tom No, I must go back and get it. I had them set aside a wonderful wine – I'll only be quarter of an hour.

Tom jumps up and walks slowly towards the passageway. It is clear that he has had to leave as he finds the discussion unbearable.

Charles Oh, but . . .

Tom	And I'm early anyway, aren't I?
Virginia	We think it's nice that you're early, Tom – it gives us a chance to be with you. *(she means this but, glancing at her husband then back at Tom, she knows it is better for him to go to recover himself)*
Tom	*(in a panic)* Yes, yes. But . . . look . . . I really must do this. I won't be long.
Virginia	That's fine, Tom. It's okay. We'll be here, don't worry. We're not going anywhere! *(suddenly aware of her faux pas)* Oh . . . I mean . . . meant . . .
Tom	Back in fifteen. *(exits)*
Virginia	Oh shit.
Charles	What?
Virginia	Oh shit, Charles, we're such stupid idiots.
Charles	What have we done?
Virginia	Can't you see that the poor man was just dying to leave? Oh shit, I did it again.
Charles	Did what again?
Virginia	I mentioned death again. I can't stop talking about death in front of him, one way or the other.
Charles	Well, I'm sure that . . .
Virginia	Yes – that's your bloody problem, isn't it, Charles?
Charles	What?
Virginia	Yes, what?
Charles	What? What are you talking about?
Virginia	Nothing, Charles, nothing you would possibly understand.

Charles	*(bewildered but trying to put on an optimistic face)* Okay, dear. I'm dense. Just dense old Charlie. But we got a party here – a difficult one. And Will and Wanda will be coming any minute now.
Virginia	*(softening)* I'm sorry. I'm just in a state. I don't know why. It's not as if we were all that close to them. Come and help me in the kitchen. What do you think he meant by saying he actually saw her, that he chased her onto an estate? You don't think . . . you don't think he's gone looking for her again? Do you?
Charles	He can look all he likes, Ginny, but she's gone. When you're dead, you're gone.
Virginia	I suppose so.

They get up and exit stage left, passing through a curtain that leads to the kitchen.

Scene two

There is a knock at the front door.

Charles	*(off-stage, from the kitchen)* I'll get it!

Charles enters, passes across the room, and exits by the passageway stage right.

	(off-stage) Hey! Great, great to see you.
Wanda and Will	Great to see you!

All three of them enter. Will and Wanda Menses are both in their mid-forties. Will, a lawyer, is dressed in a dark suit with a blue shirt and a dark tie, as if he has come from work. Wanda is wearing a stylish black dress with necklace and bracelets. They are clearly better off than the Flounts.

Wanda	Where's Ginny?

Charles	In the kitchen.
Wanda	Where else! *(laughing)*
Virginia	*(off-stage, from the kitchen)* I heard that!
Will	So . . .
Charles	Come and sit down.

Charles is rather commanding and the Menses sit obediently on the sofa. Wanda and Will cannot see Virginia as she enters the room behind them. Virginia seems momentarily at a loss, but then tiptoes to the side of the sofa and Wanda catches sight of her.

Wanda	There you are!

Wanda gets up and gives Virginia an unusually long hug. Virginia is moved, though a bit taken aback. She moves along to Will, who is standing with arms open, and they hug briefly. They all sit down, beaming at each other.

Virginia	Oh Wanda, what a relief to see you.
Will	A relief? *(a bit of a stickler for language, Will says this as if more interested in catching Virginia out than in comprehending what she really intends to say)*
Virginia	*(confused)* Yes, well . . .
Charles	Oh, she's so hard on herself! *(laughs, but is embarrassed by Virginia's awkwardness)*
Wanda	What's up, dear?
Virginia	Oh, it's nothing. It's . . . well . . . you know . . . Tom's here.
Wanda and Will	*(startled, looking around as if they have missed him)* Where?
Virginia	No, not here, not now. But he was here . . . He's gone and will be back.
Charles	Poor chap – forgot his wine.

Will	Oh shit.
All (except Will)	What?
Will	Oh, I didn't mean to startle you all. No. I just forgot to bring wine.
Charles	Oh God, Will, forget it.
Will	I had such a good Côtes-du-Rhône. A 2000 – their best year ever.
Virginia	Another time.
Wanda	He didn't bring it because he can't bear to give it away. You're a tightwad, Will, a flagrant tightwad.

Wanda's comment is dark and strangely angry. The group is shocked, and Will is upset and embarrassed.

Will	That's not true. I . . .
Wanda	*(changing topic vigorously)* Anyway. How is Tom?
Charles	He's, well . . . I think . . . *(rubs hands together, inarticulate and awkward)*
Wanda	*(looking at Virginia)* Virginia? How is he?
Virginia	Well, I think he's in great pain. We asked if he thought about her and he said that he dreams in red.
Wanda	Her hair . . .
Virginia	Yes, exactly, and he hears her voice.
Will	She talked like a sex goddess.
Charles	*(laughing)* My God, that's the truth!
Virginia	It's so hard to know what to say. But . . . he also thinks he sees her. I don't think it's, you know, like a metaphor or anything. I think he actually believes it. He said he saw her just a bit before he arrived here and he ran after her to

an estate, where she disappeared. He seemed so calm when he was saying this, so . . . you know, okay in a way, but it's weird, don't you think?

Wanda   Poor man, it must be some particular type of grief response, I suppose. I mean, Charles, you're the cognitive therapist – have you ever heard of people actually following someone they think is their departed loved one?

Charles   Um, no – not that I can recall. I mean, not in actuality. Tom thinks he actually saw her, he thinks he was following a real version of her, not like a ghost or anything like that. It kind of has me stumped.

Wanda   When did Antonia die?

Virginia   Only three weeks ago.

Wanda   That's very close. Very close.

Virginia   Yes.

Wanda   For him, she must be still here. Somewhere around here, don't you think?

Virginia   I . . .

Charles   Well . . . ah . . .

It is clear that Wanda's comment has confused the Flounts. They are not quite sure whether Wanda is referring to metaphoric or actual presence. Will can see this and steps in.

Will   I think we should move on to something else, because . . .

Wanda   *(angrily)* Because what, Will?

Will   Because he'll know we've been talking about him when he returns.

Will does not actually know why he has said this and he casts an angry glance at Wanda. It is evident that he had simply been trying to change the topic. His argument to follow will be a psychological one, and as he proceeds he will look mostly at Charles, who will look awkwardly at his feet as he senses that his expertise is not up to Will's theory.

All (except   Oh.
Will)

Will   It'll be all over our faces. We won't be able to erase her from his view. It will only make things worse. We wear what we think in our expression, you know. We may believe we don't, as thinking is such a horrible thing, but we can't fool anyone who sees us after we've been thinking about them.

Wanda   That's nonsense, Will. You have no idea what I'm thinking about you, have you?

Will   What, now? No. But it's not a matter of speculating – it doesn't work like that. The thought-about person has to be absent. You're speaking in my presence, so I obviously think I know from your expressions what you think about what I'm saying, or about me. But if I were absent and then returned, I could also tell from the expressions on your face if you'd just been thinking about me, and that's different.

Wanda   It sounds ridiculous to me.

Virginia starts to fidget and she looks anxiously at Charles. He does not return her gaze, although when she is not looking at him he glances at her and sees her distress.

Will   If you left, you would wonder what we thought about you in your absence. You would not be there to mediate, to be both you as you wished to be and you as I thought you, or as Virginia thought you. When you're absent you have no choice – everything is up for grabs. I could do whatever I wanted with you.

Virginia   *(sincere but confused)* Everything?

Will gets up, grabs the olive dish and walks about offering olives to the group. He speaks slowly, with increased authority; it is clear to him and to others that his argument is becoming increasingly extreme.

Will   In my mind. I could do anything to her in my mind that I wanted to. I could put her on a horse jumping a hedge, I could put her in military uniform going off to war, I could put her under water . . . er . . . I could . . .

Wanda   Why don't you sit down, Will.

Will sits down in another chair, looking at the others, somewhat taken by what he has said, but also aware that he is out on a limb. Wanda speaks icily and slowly, looking at Virginia.

              What he means is that he could murder me if he wished.

The group is silent for a moment.

Charles   *(anxious and unclear about what is transpiring)* Er, murder?

Will   *(speaking in a neutral, detached manner, as if explaining something to a client)* She means in my mind. If I wanted to murder her in my mind, I could. But if you do that to someone, if you've thought it, and they return in the flesh, then they have a sense of it. So we don't want to go talking on about Tom or he'll return and see that we've been talking about him.

Suddenly a woman and a man can be heard quarrelling in the street outside. The man is repeatedly yelling 'I've had it with you, sis' and the woman is shouting 'I won't be treated like that . . . Don't you dare raise your hand to me . . . And don't you dare call me sis.' The group all look at the window and are paralysed.

Charles   My God.

Will   Sounds serious. *(they all go to the window and look out)*

Charles   Maybe it's just a passing quarrel.

Virginia   She sounds frightened.

Wanda	I can't see anything. Can anyone see them?
Virginia	No, I can't see them. Where are they?
Will	I don't know where they are, but it doesn't sound good.
Wanda	What should we do?
Charles	Maybe they'll go away.
Virginia	Charles – someone may be in real danger!
Charles	Maybe we should call the police.
Will	It could be too late for that.
Wanda	I still can't see anything.

The woman's voice cries out several times: 'Get your hands off me!'

Virginia	What . . . ?
Will	I think the guy is attacking her.
Virginia and Wanda	Oh my God.
Charles	He could be armed. Look, there they are! Over there. *(points to the right)* What's he holding in his right hand?
Wanda	I can't see – what is it?
Charles	It looks like a large knife.
Virginia	What can we do?

The woman is heard yelling 'leave me alone, put that away, please put that away.' Will rushes from the room by the passageway stage right, and the door slams behind him.

Wanda	Will, where are you going?
Charles	I . . . *(walks towards the passageway but returns, clearly frightened)* I . . . I . . . I . . .
Virginia	Charles, call the police.

Wanda   Oh, it's Will.

Virginia   Where?

Wanda   Going up to them.

Virginia   *(muttering)* Oh, be careful, Will. Be careful, Will.

Wanda   Oh my God, he's run off!

Charles   Will's run off?

Virginia   No, you idiot, the bastard who's attacking the woman.

Wanda   What's Will doing?

Virginia   He's rushing her along.

Wanda   I think he may be trying to get her to safety.

Virginia   You don't suppose he'd bring her here, do you?

Wanda   *(like Virginia, suddenly worried about this possibility)* Will is very protective. He might do that. Yes, it's possible.

Virginia   Oh well . . .

They all move away from the window and stand in the middle of the room.

Charles   I'll get another glass. *(leaves for the kitchen)*

Wanda   *(to herself)* Yes, he might do that . . .

Wanda and Virginia, as if in a kind of trance, also walk towards the kitchen and exit.

Act two

Scene one

Wanda and Virginia are seated on the sofa, passing the olives. There is a knock at the front door and Charles enters from the kitchen and passes through the room, on his way to open the door. Wanda and Virginia rise and look with anxiety to their right. In doing so, Virginia spills some olives and bends down to pick them up, but Wanda is too absorbed to notice. They wait in silence.

Charles   *(off-stage)* Oh, good, good.

Will enters with his arms around a woman in her early twenties. She is wearing a black leather suit with a skirt and has vivid red hair. Charles follows. Wanda gasps on first sight of the woman; Virginia is still trying to find olives, but when she looks up, her mouth falls open and she drops the olives again.

Will   *(leading the woman into the centre of the room)* It's going to be okay. This is Charles. And . . . Charles . . . ? *(looks around and can't see Charles, who is behind him)*

Charles   Here, Will, I'm right here.

Will   Oh good. There you are. Good man. Now . . . uh . . . *(looking at Virginia and Wanda)* The two women here are my wife and Charles's wife, Wanda and Virginia . . . and . . .

Wanda smiles but can't say anything and Virginia is still picking up olives.

Clarissa	*(somewhat shy, but strangely direct for a woman who has just endured an assault)* Hi.
Will	I think . . . I'm sorry, I don't know your name.
Clarissa	Clarissa.
Will	I think Clarissa has had a terrible shock and we . . .
Virginia	Why don't you sit down, dear.

Virginia moves over to Clarissa. She almost has to wrestle her away from Will, then leads her to the sofa, where she puts Clarissa between herself and Wanda. Charles and Will remain standing. Wanda smiles and then hands Clarissa a glass of water, finally shaking herself into speech.

Wanda	Yes, do sit and just drink this and . . .
Clarissa	I don't want to be any trouble . . .
Charles	Oh no. No. No trouble.
Wanda	*(crisply)* Sit down, Will.

Will and Charles look around for chairs and sit down.

Virginia	You poor thing.

Clarissa drinks her glass of water slowly and gazes around the room as she does so. They all remain silent, in some shock, and Clarissa slumps in a sort of coy chuckle as she sips more water.

Wanda	*(as if suddenly understanding something)* My God.
Virginia	*(almost simultaneously)* Yes – my God.
Clarissa	*(frightened)* What?
Wanda	Oh. It's just that . . . It's just that you bear an uncanny, a striking . . .
Virginia	. . . resemblance to a friend of ours . . .
Wanda	. . . to a friend who died just three weeks ago.
Virginia	Yes, the same red hair and blue eyes . . .

Will	. . . and the voice.
Virginia	You SOUND like her.
Wanda	It's amazing. It's . . .
Clarissa	I don't know about this. I . . . *(she begins to get up)*
Virginia	Oh, dear, no, don't . . .
Wanda	No, you've just been through . . .
Will	That, uh, that was her former partner out there.
Charles	*(to Clarissa)* What, the one hitting you?

Clarissa moves her hands above her head, as if clearing a mental space. She is quiet for a moment and then speaks slowly, clearly distressed.

Clarissa	I wouldn't call him my partner. I don't even know him really, although he seems to think he knows me. *(looks around the room at each of the others, searching their faces)* He comes up to me just after I left the pub and starts going on about how I'm some ho' and where have I been. I didn't know what he was going on about.
Charles	You don't know him?
Clarissa	Maybe . . . but if I do . . . Well, it's complicated.

There is an awkward pause as the other characters look at one another and then concentrate on objects around the room, clearly confused about what they have got themselves into.

Virginia	You don't have to tell us if you don't . . .
Wanda	. . . want to.
Will	*(eager to change the subject)* It's none of our business.
Clarissa	No, it's not that. It's just a complicated thing to tell.
Charles	Complicated because . . . ?
Clarissa	Well, it's sort of hard to believe and stuff . . .

Virginia	It's okay, you really don't have to tell us. It must be a terrible shock to have a stranger come up to you like that and start attacking you.
Clarissa	Yeah, it is. But part of the complication is that everyone is sort of a stranger.
Wanda	Everyone, dear?
Clarissa	That's part of the complication.
Virginia	Charles, do you want to go to the kitchen and bring something to drink?
Will	Yes, good idea. *(to Clarissa)* Would you like a touch of . . .
Wanda	Whiskey. Just a little. It will help.
Virginia	Did he hurt you?
Clarissa	I don't know. I don't think so.
Wanda	Look. Oh poor dear. How thoughtless of us. Here we are pummelling you – sorry! *(embarrassed)* – with questions I mean and . . . let's go to the bathroom and have a clean up.

She leads Clarissa by the hand towards the bathroom, which is through the passageway stage right. Both Charles and Will watch Clarissa walking across the room. She is stunningly beautiful. After Wanda and Clarissa have left, Will, Charles and Virginia jump up and meet in the middle of the room in a huddle, talking softly.

Virginia	My God, what are we going to do?
Will	I agree, this is a problem.
Charles	I can get her some whiskey if . . .
Virginia	Charles, concentrate. For God's sake, pay attention. She's the spitting image of Antonia.
Will	It is astonishing. She could be her twin sister.

Charles   Well, shall we call the police?

Will   Charles . . . I . . .

Virginia   Charles, you idiot. What for?

Charles   Well, can't they deal with her?

Will   No, Charles, she's okay. She can file a crime report later, anyway. I don't think the guy will come back.

Charles   Well, Ginny, what's the problem?

Virginia   Tom must be minutes away. We can't have them in the same room together. She IS Antonia. He'll be . . . well . . . It's hard to imagine what he'll think.

Charles   Well, can't we tell him what happened?

Virginia   What difference will that make?

Charles   I should have thought that being told what happened will be important. I mean, he won't think that we arranged this or anything, will he?

Virginia   *(slowly, exasperated)* No, Charles, he will not think we have set this up – that is not the point. He will, however, be stunned and overwhelmed by the return of his presumably dead wife!

Charles   Oh my word. IS it Antonia? Could she possibly have slipped out of the morgue before the autopsy? What should we do?

Virginia   Don't be stupid, Charles. You can't do that, can you Will?

They look at Will anxiously.

Will   Extremely unlikely. No, I think this is someone else – although I couldn't swear to it.

Charles   Ginny, we must think what to do.

Virginia   Yes, I . . .

She breaks off as they hear Wanda and Clarissa returning. They are all standing awkwardly in the middle of the room. Clarissa has her hair up and she has taken off her jacket to reveal a top that shows plenty of cleavage.

Oh, good. Oh – you look lovely, Clarissa.

Charles   Yes, stunning.

Wanda   Now, where's that whiskey?

Charles   Oh, coming up! *(races out of the room to the kitchen)*

Virginia   Come and sit down.

They all sit down: Clarissa and Will in chairs, Virginia and Wanda on the sofa.

Clarissa   I'm sorry to be such trouble.

Virginia   It's no trouble at all, dear. You've been through a terrible ordeal. You need to collect yourself.

Charles rushes back into the room, hands Clarissa a glass of whiskey with ice and stands back, gawking at her.

Thank you, Charles. *(points to a chair on the opposite side of the room)* You can sit down now, darling.

Clarissa   I shouldn't be causing such trouble for all of you.

Will   It's not a problem.

Virginia   Yes, we're just waiting to have a bit of dinner and there's no hurry.

Charles   Yes, there's no hurry. In fact *(stands)* you must stay for dinner!

Clarissa   Oh, I don't . . .

Virginia   That's a bit presumptuous of you, isn't it, Charles? Clarissa may well have other plans for the evening.

Wanda	Yes, how dare we hijack you, my dear! You must have had enough of strangers in the night!
Clarissa	No, I have no plans. That's not it. It's just not right. You're all here for another reason than being with me.
Charles	No, that's not true.
Virginia	My dear Clarissa, if you WISH to stay, of course that's . . .
Wanda	Yes, of course that would be . . .
Will	It's for you to say. *(looks at the women awkwardly)*
Clarissa	It's terribly nice of you.
Charles	Think nothing of it, Clarissa.
Clarissa	You can call me Rissa.
Will	As in 'risen'?
Clarissa	Huh?
Wanda	Will, for God's sake.
Will	It just came out.
Virginia	We . . . we . . .
Charles	We just need to set another place.
Clarissa	But you seem to have already set me a place.
Charles	Predestined!
Will	Foreordained!
Virginia	Don't mind the boys, Rissa. We do have another guest, and he should be here any minute.
Clarissa	Oh, then . . .
Charles	Nonsense.
Virginia	Whatever do you mean, 'nonsense', Charles?

Will   Ginny, I think Charles sensed that Rissa might object . . .

Clarissa   I really don't think I should be here.

Virginia   Nonsense, my dear.

Charles   *(very angry)* Why the hell is it that you can say 'nonsense' but I can't?

Clarissa recoils and puts her hand over her face.

Wanda   Oh, poor darling. Charles, you've given her a fright.

Virginia   She doesn't need the sight of another violent man, does she?

Will   I think we should just calm down. It's been a terrible shock for us all.

Charles   *(sitting down, sheepish)* I'm terribly sorry, Rissa. It's incredibly insensitive of me. It's just that sometimes I don't think my meaning is understood, or . . .

Clarissa   It's okay, Charles. You're a sweet person. I can tell. It's not what you think. It wasn't your voice or manner that upset me, it's just that it reminded me of the strange man who seemed to think I was his wife or his sister or something. *(pauses, puts her head in her hands and lowers her voice)* It has to do with the complication I was telling you about.

Virginia   Rissa, why don't we take the time and you tell us.

Clarissa   Are you sure?

Virginia   *(looking around the room)* I think we're sure, aren't we?

Will   *(anxious and tentative)* Rissa, it's not something we'll regret hearing – if I may put it that way – is it?

Clarissa   That's . . . hard to answer. I . . . I don't . . . know.

Wanda   *(irritated)* What do you MEAN, Will?

Will   *(puffed up, as if giving a seminar; Wanda raises her hands in despair)* Well – and forgive me for a moment, Clarissa, but

123

Wanda wants me to clarify this, so . . . If Clarissa's 'complication' includes involvement in a crime, however unwitting or tangential, then once we are informed of such a crime, we could be accessories to the fact.

Charles   Well . . . perhaps we really should have the police present.

Will   No, Charles, I meant this as an example, not as an ACTUAL worry about what Clarissa is going to tell us.

Wanda   Well, Will, if it isn't actual then what is it?

Will   It's a theoretical possibility.

Wanda   Why, may I ask, at a time like this, do you find it necessary to talk to us about theoretical possibilities? Can't you see that this is a real situation, not some case being discussed in a law seminar?

Will   (slowly, as if to a child) Wanda, my love, the reason we theorise is in order to prepare ourselves for reality. If we think about what Clarissa might be about to say, then we can better understand the options we have for helping her and for helping ourselves at the same time.

Wanda   Jesus, you sound like some wet politician!

Clarissa   It's nothing to do with crime. I don't think so.

Will   You don't think so?

Clarissa   No, I don't think the complication has to do with crime . . . but I can't be sure.

Will   So . . . we may not, after all, want to hear about your complication?

Clarissa   Well, I'm not sure. I hadn't thought about it in that way.

Will   Remember, everyone, this was only an example, but . . . well . . . (looks earnestly at Clarissa) Surely you must know whether or not you've committed a crime?

Charles	What do you mean by a 'crime', Will? Rissa may not know what you mean.
Will	I mean breaking the law.
Charles	Oh.
Virginia	But failure to pay one's parking tickets is breaking the law. Are you including that, Will? Would we be accessories to the fact if she tells us about unpaid parking tickets?
Will	Possibly.
Wanda	Lawyers! You're all a complete pain.
Will	It's possible that we could be found guilty of complicity.
Wanda	Will, if Rissa hasn't paid parking tickets all her life – if she owes the government £15,000 in unpaid tickets – surely we aren't going to be prosecuted by the Crown Prosecution Service if we know about it?
Will	It's theoretically possible. But Clarissa could also sue us.
Charles	What? Well . . . perhaps we should bring the police in on this – I have been saying that, you know.
Virginia	Charles, you'd have thought that being a cognitive therapist, you could at least have learned to keep your mouth shut.
Charles	My profession seeks solutions to problems.
Virginia	Well, your PROFESSION may do, but YOU are another matter altogether.
Will	Ginny, Ginny, Ginny . . .
Clarissa	I don't want to cause trouble.
Virginia	I'm sorry, Rissa, love.
Wanda	*(to Will)* So?
Will	Well, if Rissa were found to have committed a crime by

not paying her bill and if she pleaded that she told four people of her crime, one of whom was a cognitive therapist, then she could sue Charles on the ground that he did not take note of her admission, which, it could be argued, was tantamount to a cry for help.

Charles   But she's not my client, is she, Will?

Will   Nor is the suicidal guy who says he intends to jump off the building that day, but if it can be shown that he knew you were a therapist and then told you of his plan, his clinical requirement hired you in that moment and you were then obliged to look after him.

Charles   But shouldn't the police be . . .

Virginia   Charles!

At this point everyone is clearly uncomfortable. Virginia gets up and passes around a few canapés and Wanda becomes preoccupied with taking lint off her clothing.

Clarissa   Will – may I call you that?

Will   Of course.

Wanda   *(chillingly)* It is his name, dear, go for it.

Clarissa   I don't know.

Will   Don't know?

Clarissa   It's such a lovely name. Like 'will' . . . you know what I mean?

Clarissa is now talking to herself, in a dream-like state. She is in an evolving rhapsody.

Like W-I-L-L. You came to my rescue. You willed it, didn't you? You just showed up – a stranger. A lot nicer than that other stranger. The one who called me . . . what did he call me? I can't remember the name. It was something like 'Ronnie'. I don't know. Who knows? Who knows anything? You see, that's my complication. I can't know. Let me show you.

Clarissa stands up, gathering her skirt up to her hips. There are audible gasps from all in the group. Both men stare at her revealed underwear and the women look away. Clarissa reaches into her knickers and removes a piece of paper.

I keep this letter here for safe keeping.

Clarissa sits down again as she unfolds the paper.

Wanda   *(sarcastically, clearly becoming less well-disposed towards Clarissa)* Well, dear, I wonder just how safe it would be there!

Clarissa   *(as if she has not heard Wanda)* This is what I can say to you. Well, actually, it's not me speaking. It's entitled 'Med Alert' and it says . . . *(clears throat)* . . . it says: 'Clarissa was hit by a bus on April 5th and was in a coma for nine months. She has regained all her intellectual functioning but is without any memory of her past. Indeed the hospital named her Clarissa – we are unsure of her true identity. Anyone who has need for further clarification in this matter can contact Dr Anthony Sprecht at the Medici Hospital, on 020 7207 7777.'

Virginia   You were hit by a bus?

Clarissa   So they say.

Will   But you don't remember?

Clarissa   No. Not really.

Will   Not really, or not at all?

Clarissa   I have something there, you know, something that is sort of there . . . but it just won't come up, if you know what I mean.

Virginia   Kind of like a computer that has the information but you just can't get it to come up on the screen?

Clarissa   Yeah, it's sort of like that.

Virginia   *(transfixed)* Go on.

Clarissa   Well, Dr Sprecht is a very nice man. And he told me that I should carry this note around with me in the event of need. I think he said something about 'unforeseen circumstances'. Anyway, in the last three weeks I've been released from hospital, I have a home, a place to live that social services provided, and I have a little money. I don't know what I did.

Charles   What you did?

Clarissa   I mean, I don't know what sort of work I did. I don't think I have committed a crime but, as you can imagine, I can't really account for anything.

Charles   Um. You know, I've read these studies – I'm a cognitive therapist, you know – and these studies show how we can intervene with ideas to redirect dilemmas into solutions.

Clarissa   Er . . .

Charles   We, well, we come up with a mental solution.

Wanda   A solution?

Charles   Yes, you know, something that you can say to yourself – a statement – that redirects your mental pathway.

Will   So Clarissa should do what?

Charles   Well, uh, let me think a bit. *(puts his head in his hands for 30 seconds)* I'm sorry, but as of this moment I can't think of anything. *(the whole group slumps with disappointment)* No, wait a minute. Wait a minute. First, Clarissa, let me ask you a few questions.

Will   Do that, Charles, and she becomes your client.

Charles   Sorry?

Will	If you do, then she is your client.
Charles	What, because I ask her a few questions?
Will	No, because you are a therapist and therefore doing so constitutes a professional action.
Charles	Well, ah . . .
Virginia	That was a bit of cognitive therapy, eh, Charles?
Charles	What, Virginia?
Virginia	*(triumphantly)* You want me to spell it out? What Will said to you put a redirecting idea into your mind, didn't it? You can't ask Clarissa questions because of your role.
Charles	How about you, then?
Virginia	Me?
Charles	Yes, you. Surely an architect can ask whatever questions she likes?
Virginia	'Town planner', Charles.
Charles	Originally an architect, now a town planner. You go ahead, you ask.
Virginia	I have no questions.
Charles	*(enjoying this moment, getting his own back)* You have no questions?
Virginia	Well, Charles, Clarissa isn't a town, now, is she? So I'm no expert.
Charles	But if she were?
Virginia	What?
Charles	If she were a town, what questions would you ask?
Virginia	That's absurd.

Charles   No, Virginia, it's cognitive therapy. I have given you a redirecting idea – like 'don't think of flying elephants'. Once it's in your mind it's a force with a future, that will, that will . . .

Virginia   No, Charles, I don't think you have it right.

Charles stands up threateningly but then collapses down again, deflated.

Charles   Cognitive therapy works. That's all I have to say.

There is an embarrassed silence. Then a knock at the front door.

Virginia   Oh my God, it's Tom.

Act three

Scene one

The characters are in exactly the same positions as at the close of the last act, as if they had been freeze-framed. There are two or three knocks at the door. The knocking becomes more insistent, but at first nobody moves. Then Virginia gets up and walks almost ceremonially into the passageway stage right. She returns a few seconds later, with Tom following behind. He holds a large bouquet of flowers in his right hand, and a bottle of wine and chocolates in his left hand. He walks forward, hidden by the flowers, and is unable to see the group. He stops in the middle of the room.

Virginia   *(strained)* Oh, Tom, love, oh, you needn't have. Those wonderful flowers – it's as though you've brought us a magical garden!

Tom   It's okay.

Virginia   Tom, I . . .

Tom   Yes . . . ?

Tom follows Virginia into the room. They stop and Virginia steps back to stand next to Tom and gently puts her hand on his arm. They are some ten feet from the group, who are sitting with their heads down – except for Clarissa, who starts to rise to her feet.

Virginia   Tom, I'm sorry, but . . .

Tom	*(false laugh)* Ginny, it's okay. The walk did me good. There's nothing to worry about. And here I am in the Garden of Eden, reborn . . . ready for anything.
Clarissa	*(almost inaudible)* Ready for anything.
Tom	Huh?
Virginia	You, I . . .
Tom	Anyway . . . what's a guy got to do to get out of the garden? Can someone take these? And I have wine and chocolates!
Clarissa	Chocolates?
Tom	Virginia?
Virginia	No. *(pauses)* Here, let me.

Tom lifts the bouquet of flowers up high over his head, so he can see where he is going. He looks around the room and smiles wanly as he sees Will, Wanda and Charles. He even 'sees' Clarissa, but then as he looks at her again, he drops the wine and the chocolates, and Virginia darts forward to catch the flowers. His gaze is fixed on Clarissa, who is just a few feet from him.

Tom	*(to Clarissa)* You!
Charles	Whoops!
Wanda	Oh Christ.
Clarissa	What lovely flowers.

Tom and Clarissa are now inside some kind of mutual hypnosis. The others watch and comment, but as if they are witnesses to something over which they have no influence.

Tom	*(softly)* Holy . . . shit.

Virginia quietly walks across the room to join all the others, who have moved imperceptibly towards the kitchen door. This leaves Clarissa and

*Tom to occupy the centre of the stage. As the other members of the cast
speak, they do so as if part of a Greek chorus.*

Clarissa   They're lovely.

Tom   Yes.

Clarissa   What . . . is your name?

Tom   Tom . . . You don't . . . you don't know my name?

Clarissa   Do I know you?

Tom   Yes.

Virginia   Tom . . . I think . . .

Charles   *(formally, as if he wants to penetrate Tom's trance with cold
                hard facts)* Tom, meet Clarissa. She was attacked by a
                stranger in the street and Will came to her rescue. She was
                in an accident a year ago and has lost her memory. She
                may stay for dinner.

Tom   No. It's impossible.

Virginia   Tom, look before you.

Tom   I am.

Will   Tom, she's a stranger. You don't know her.

Tom   Yes, I do.

*Tom is looking at Clarissa, deeply, lovingly. Clarissa walks up to Tom and
they are within touching distance.*

                Do I know you?

Clarissa   Yes.

Will   *(trying to bring Clarissa out of her spell)* But Clarissa, how is
                this possible? Minutes ago, you remembered nothing. You
                didn't even know whether or not you had committed a
                crime. How can you say you remember him?

Clarissa	I didn't say I remembered him, I said I knew him.
Virginia	*(alarmed)* How is this possible?
Clarissa	I don't know.
Tom	I do.
Wanda	Tom, hold on.
Tom	Why?
Wanda	Because you're deeply vulnerable and we all know what you're thinking.
Tom	How can you know?
Wanda	Tom, we all know she could be Antonia's twin. We all saw this in the beginning.

When Wanda speaks 'Antonia', Tom shudders. Up till now he has been looking only at Clarissa, but now, as if brought out of a trance by the name of his deceased wife, he looks at the group and he is angry.

Tom	You arranged this?
Wanda	No, of course not. It's an accident.
Tom	Exactly!
Wanda	Exactly?
Will	I think what Tom means is that this IS an accident. I can see that he would believe that Antonia has returned as Clarissa.

Will leads the group from its isolated position and they now walk to stage centre, forming a semicircle around Tom and Clarissa.

Virginia	Don't be absurd!
Will	I only meant . . .
Wanda	It's an absurd legal postulation, just game-playing, and now it's going too far.

Virginia	They don't know each other. They have only met.
Tom	Do I know you?
Clarissa	Yes.
Tom	Do you know me?
Clarissa	Yes.
Tom	Do you have a mole shaped like a heart on the inside of your left thigh?
Clarissa	Yes.
Tom	May I see it?
Clarissa	Of course – it is yours.

She pulls up her skirt and once again both Charles and Will are riveted to her body. But it is to Tom that she reveals her thigh, and as she leans forward she puts her hand on his head to steady herself. Tom falls on his knee and kisses the mole. He rises very slowly and puts a hand on each of her shoulders. Then they move in a very slow circle, gazing at one another. The other members of the group alternate between looking at the moving couple, at one another, out of the window, and towards the passageway, stage right. They are trapped between being embarrassed and being paralysed with uncertainty.

Tom	I think we need to be alone.

He lets go of Clarissa and stands next to her, body to body. She has her arm wrapped around his waist. They face the others, who are still organised in a semicircle.

Will	I'm not sure that's a good idea.
Tom	I have questions.
Virginia	What sort of questions?
Tom	They are private questions.
Will	Tom, we can't leave you alone. Clarissa has been through a nightmare, we can't just . . .

135

Wanda	What Will means is that you've both been through trauma and we don't think it's a good idea to . . .
Charles	Let the blind lead the blind?
Wanda	*(wincing)* We don't think it's a good idea for two people in such a vulnerable state of mind to be alone with each other, not for now.
Tom	What about my questions?
Will	Can you ask them in our presence?
Tom	That would be difficult.
Clarissa	Tom?
Tom	*(drawn by her voice as if by a hand, he now looks directly at Clarissa)* Yes, love?
Clarissa	What do you want to know?
Tom	These are private matters – I should really ask you alone, but my friends . . .
Clarissa	Go ahead, it's okay, you ask what you like.

Tom clears his throat and pinches his nose nervously, trying to compose himself. He releases Clarissa and stands back a couple of feet.

Tom	Let's see, when did we first meet?
Clarissa	About . . . fifteen minutes ago?
Tom	Not before?
Clarissa	I might not know.
Tom	Because you've lost your memory?
Clarissa	Yes, I'm told I was in an accident and I was in a coma for nine months. I was released from hospital three weeks ago.
Tom	Three weeks?
Clarissa	Yes, the 13th.

Tom	The 13th?
Clarissa	The 13th.
Tom	Antonia died on the 13th. She . . . uh . . . she died.
Clarissa	I'm so sorry.
Tom	Yes. Thank you. She was wonderful. She, uh, she . . . You look . . . You could be her double. You could be her. I mean, it's not just uncanny, it's as if you ARE her.
Clarissa	How confusing.
Tom	No. Yes. No, it's wonderful. It's as if you've come back.
Wanda	Tom, I . . .
Will	Let them go on.
Tom	It's unbelievable to see you again. I never thought I would see you again. I've been dreaming about you, though, every night. Every night.
Clarissa	That's odd.
Tom	Odd?
Clarissa	I felt that someone had been dreaming me.
Tom	You did?
Clarissa	Yes, it's a peculiar feeling. I was asleep, you know, for a very long time. And I can remember my dreams. Dreams about living in another place, but a familiar place, a working mill house next to a fast-moving stream, the water flowing over the rocks . . .
Tom	In a forest with lots of cypress trees that opened onto a vast field . . .
Clarissa	. . . of daffodils that never died. That were always in bloom.
Tom	I know this dream.

Clarissa	You do? How?
Tom	I don't know. I haven't dreamt it, but I know it.
Clarissa	Yes, you knew about the cypress trees and the field.
Tom	And it's always May there, the month of May.
Clarissa	Yes. How do we know the same dream?
Tom	I don't know. I . . . you were saying, though, that you were being dreamed by someone.
Clarissa	Yes. I heard someone calling for me, someone from across the field, someone who I thought was hailing me or crying, and so I walked through the field and it was a man's voice.
Tom	Did you see him?
Clarissa	No. I felt him though. It was as if he found me first and just carried me off with him. He kept talking to me but I only heard the sound of his voice, not the words, not until I opened my eyes and it was Dr Sprecht who was there and he was talking to me.
Tom	Dr Sprecht.
Clarissa	My doctor at the Medici Hospital.
Tom	The Medici? You were at the Medici?
Clarissa	For ten months.
Tom	That's where my Antonia died. She died there. You were in the same hospital. You were . . . what wing . . . do you remember the wing?
Clarissa	The East Wing, fourth floor, room 422.
Tom	Room 422? Are you sure?
Clarissa	*(looking alarmed)* Yes. Is there something wrong?
Tom	Antonia was in 421.

Clarissa	Next door?
Tom	Yes, right next door. I mean – the doctors, the nurses, someone must have noticed the uncanny similarity between the two of you. Why wouldn't they have said something or done something?
Virginia	Tom, what could they have done?
Tom	Well, Virginia, look at her. They're like twins. If two women looking identical to one another were one room apart in the same hospital, don't you think someone would have said something?
Virginia	Like what, Tom?
Tom	Well, like . . . like . . . like 'Look, we know you're suffering and you're going to lose her, but we have something to show you, something to uplift your spirits. There's a woman in the next room who is identical to your wife, someone who could be her, someone who was asleep but is now awake.' Or . . . I don't know . . . I might have overheard one nurse talking to another saying how amazing it was . . .
Will	I agree with you, Tom. I think it's odd something wasn't said.
Tom	Yes, and why not? Why not? Except they knew this was the uncanny. They knew something sacred was happening, something beyond the ordinary, something out of their grasp, something they dare not interfere with, something . . .
Charles	But if they'd told you who was in room 422 and brought her to see you, wouldn't that be rather like . . . a . . . sort of a transplant?
Virginia	Oh Christ, Charles.
Charles	*(looking at Will)* Would it have been legal, Will? If they knew one woman looked exactly like another and one was

in a coma, they couldn't have introduced them, could they? What if Clarissa woke up to find that while she was asleep they had married her to a man who insisted on the transplant?

Will   *(walking around scratching his head)* Well, Charles has a point, Tom . . . I don't think they could have actually brought the two of you together if they KNOWINGLY thought, much less wrote down, that doing so was an effort to give you a transplant for a wife. Because in Clarissa's condition, we can see that she is deeply impressionable and thinks she knows you as it is, and . . . well . . .

Charles Indeed, but Will, are we legally implicated here? Are we accessories to a fact? Should we be notifying social services? I mean, isn't Clarissa on the verge of being abducted by Tom? In fact, you brought her in here, shouldn't we put her back on the street?

Virginia My God, you are a coward, Charles. That would be absurd. She's still in shock. Look at the poor thing!

Clarissa has left Tom's side and is now walking around the room, speaking slowly and softly to herself.

Clarissa . . . like out of a dream.

Tom   *(adopting the pace of Clarissa's speech)* Yes, like out of a dream.

Clarissa Dr Sprecht said I spoke in my dreams.

Tom   I expect you did.

Clarissa He said that I kept saying 'Mr Henders, I can't keep up with you if you walk so fast' and that later I added 'Mr Henders, can you hold my hand for a moment?'

All (except My God.
Tom and
Clarissa)

Clarissa   What's the matter?

She stops, alarmed, and Tom rushes to her side, holding her hand.

Tom   My name is Henders. Tom Henders.

Clarissa   It is?

Tom   Yes. It's my name. You were dreaming about me. I was coming to collect you.

Will   Tom, I think this is . . .

Virginia   This is all too much for us to take in.

Wanda   To know how to think this without getting . . .

Charles   We need to have an idea to organise it for us.

Tom   How so?

Charles   Well, I mean we need a way to explain this to ourselves, so that we can be rational.

Tom   It's easy to see what happened.

Charles   It is?

Tom   Yes, it is.

Will   What, then?

Tom   My Antonia was dying and Clarissa arrived to take her place. God, or some divine being or logic or whatever you want to call it, came and put Clarissa close enough to me so that she began to know me, she could overhear my voice. My love of her radiated, it moved in a circle and my love and my words linked Clarissa to her doctor, who then became my agent and she moved from her coma, from her dreamland, towards me. And the red in my dreams was . . . it was . . . my vision of Clarissa coming here to meet me, to find me. *(looks at Clarissa)* And you have.

Virginia clears her throat and rises from her chair, speaking in a rather strained and over-cheery voice.

Virginia You know what? I think it's time we got some food inside us, don't you? Another setting! *(rushes off to the kitchen)*

Wanda *(jumps to her feet and clears the canapés)* Absolutely right! Let's have some dinner and then you, Tom, and you, Clarissa, can share more about yourselves. *(quickly follows Virginia to the kitchen)*

Charles Yes. We can then begin to form an idea in us of . . . well, you know, of how to make sense of all of this.

Virginia and Wanda rush back into the room, with Virginia holding a new place setting. She sets the new place as she talks.

Virginia Or not . . . it doesn't matter. I mean, it doesn't have to matter. It just is what it is, che sera sera, and we can move on.

Wanda Yes, we can move on. At least to the main course!

Virginia Yes! What a starter this has been.

All except Tom and Clarissa engage in false laughter.

Scene two

The characters are seated at the dinner table. Clarissa and Tom are in the middle, opposite one another; Virginia is next to Clarissa and opposite Will; Wanda and Charles are opposite one another. For the first few moments we hear the sound of knives and forks clinking on plates and the group is silent. Then Will suddenly pushes his seat back.

Will *(in a John Wayne voice)* Well, I just gotta say that this is one heck of a great meal, little lady!

Wanda Will? *(startled, pauses, looks around nervously at the other guests)* Oh no.

Will Now, don't you go and get worried there, Feisty Ho.

Virginia *(very anxious)* Wanda! He's gone American. What's happening . . . ?

Wanda	It's, it's . . . it's not happened in a while. It wasn't supposed to happen.
Will	*(surveying the group, beaming)* You know, I think we are fortunate to live in this great country of ours. To have right here on our plates food from our good earth.
Charles	Will, what's up?
Will	Proudfit's the name. I'm Hal Proudfit and this is my wife . . . Well, I call her Feisty Ho . . . but she's really Antonia Proudfit, or Toni Proudfit to y'all.
Tom	Antonia?
Wanda	Yes, Tom, it's one, it's . . . we've lost Will to one of his alters.
Virginia	What?
Wanda	Will is a multiple.
Virginia	A multiple of what?
Wanda	Will has different personalities. He's been on medication for twenty years and only under great stress does he lose it. I think it's the events of, you know, the last hour.
Will	This is great food. What a guest house.
Charles	*(immediately into professional mode)* Guest house?
Will	Yup, it's a great guest house. Nice food. Lucky for Toni and me that we're mixing it up with strangers. Nice folks, too. I can see that. *(turns to Clarissa and Tom)* I'm sorry, I didn't get your names.
Clarissa	I'm Clarissa.
Tom	Tom. *(they shake hands)*
Will	Yeah, well, I can tell you two are one heck of a couple. Look at that, Toni. Look at how in love they are, positively glowing. You on your honeymoon?

Tom	I . . .
Will	Ah, I knew it!
Virginia	They've only just . . .
Will	Newlyweds! I knew it. Ain't that cute. Damn, if we aren't lucky.
Wanda	Hal, dear . . .
Will	Yup?
Wanda	Hal, I think the cattle need feeding.
Will	Oh, holy cow! Holy cow. Now that's one, ain't it. Toni says the cattle need feeding. And I bless them. Wonderful creatures. Okay, hun?
Wanda	Yes, dear.
Will	Where'd we corral them?
Wanda	By the creek, about a hundred yards north from here. We really shouldn't leave them any longer without a quick check.
Will	Okay, y'all. I'll be right back.

Will gets up, salutes everyone and leaves by the passageway towards the front door, singing 'Come on little dogies'. There is a stunned silence and the group continue for some 30 seconds to move knives and forks and try to drink.

Wanda	I'm so sorry.
Virginia	Wanda, darling, why didn't you ever say anything?
Wanda	It's so, well, we thought it was in the past. It's rare nowadays.
Tom	It used to be more frequent?
Wanda	Yes, every few days and . . .

Charles	How many personalities does he have?
Wanda	I don't know, really. At least twelve steady ones and then the occasional stranger that I can't possibly make out.
Virginia	Is he safe outside?
Wanda	It's what I do. When he's Hal, I always tell him to go out and tend to the cattle and then he leaves for a bit and when he comes back, Hal is gone.
Clarissa	Maybe he just needed some fresh air?
Tom	Yeah. Just needed to escape for a moment.
Wanda	Well, that's right, in a way. But . . . it is worrying.
Virginia	Worrying?
Wanda	Oh God. *(she breaks down, sobbing, and Virginia comforts her)*
Virginia	It's all right, dear. What a terrible burden on you.
Wanda	We could be in danger.
All (except Wanda)	What?
Wanda	We could be in some danger.
Tom	Why? What could happen?
Wanda	When he returns.
Virginia	You said Hal would be gone.
Wanda	Yes, Hal will be gone, but some other alter may be in his place.
Clarissa	Like who?
Wanda	We've nothing to worry about unless it's Vladimir.
Virginia	Vladimir?

Wanda   He is terrifying. A paranoid psychotic who can be very
        threatening . . . can even . . . uh . . .

Charles Can even what?

Virginia For God's sake, Wanda, tell us.

Tom   Yes, we have to know what to do.

Wanda   If he thinks you're his enemy, he can even try to kill you.
        You have to be very quiet if it's Vladimir. You have to
        agree with everything he says and do whatever he tells you.
        If he calls you 'friend', then you're okay. It means he will
        not try to kill you. If he asks you 'what are you thinking?'
        it means he thinks you may be an enemy and he's unsure.
        If he says 'what's your problem?' it means that he has
        decided you are definitely the enemy.

Virginia Well, what can we do?

Wanda   We have to stand up as a group, all of us together, and we
        have to repeat the following statement in unison: 'You
        have the right to remain silent. You have the right to an
        attorney. Anything you say now can and will be used
        against you in a court of law. Do you understand what has
        been said to you?'

Charles Why that?

Wanda   The doctors say that he must have seen some American
        movie or television programme, or something in which
        someone who committed murder is caught and has the
        Miranda read to them. It's the American version of the
        police caution. When he hears this it makes him think he's
        already killed someone and he will stop – almost always.

Virginia Almost always?

Tom   What do you mean, almost?

Wanda   If we don't say it in unison, if one of us is quiet, then for
        some reason we don't understand it's as if the spell doesn't

146

work and then he turns on the entire group. We are all enemies.

Charles   I knew it. I think we should call the police.

Virginia   And say what?

Charles   And tell them that a guest at dinner is a multiple personality and we think he may come back as a murderer. That we might all be at risk of our lives.

Wanda   Charles, it won't work, darling.

Charles   Why not?

Wanda   They won't come. We've tried this many times before. They will only come if an incident has already occurred, as with Clarissa earlier. And even if we did call them, they would take two hours to get here and if he is Vladimir, it will be too late.

Virginia   Oh my God, what are we to do?

Wanda   Let's practise the Miranda. Repeat after me. 'You have the right to remain silent.'

The group mumbles. They are out of unison and Clarissa is not speaking.

No. That won't work. We have to say it TOGETHER and all of us have to take part. *(Wanda is now yelling at the group, clearly desperate)* Clarissa, you have to join in. Try again: 'You have the right to remain silent' . . . that's good . . . 'You have the right to an attorney' . . . better . . . 'Anything you say now can and will be used against you in a court of law. Do you understand what has been said to you?' Let's try it again.

The group repeats this three times. By the final version they are in perfect unison and are rather chuffed and overconfident.

There, that's excellent. I think that will do fine.

Virginia   How or when will we know to begin?

Wanda	My signal will be the following statement. I will say 'Vladimir Smirnoff . . .'
Charles	The vodka?
Virginia	Shut up and listen, Charles.
Wanda	'Vladimir Smirnoff, the authorities have something to say to you.' When you hear that, get ready, count to three, and then we must all say 'You have the right to remain silent . . .' and so forth. Got it?
Tom	How will you know?
Wanda	We will all know.
Virginia	Why not just say it to him immediately?
Wanda	There is a kind of rhythm to this. We have to let him be Vladimir for a while. If we try to shut down the alter too soon it will backfire.
Tom	Can't you just call him 'Hal'? Won't Hal come back?
Wanda	It doesn't work like that. I could call him 'Will', but that wouldn't work either. He has disassociated himself now – he has split into a multiple – because the stress here has meant that important parts of himself can't speak up, can't be represented. Whenever he feels this deeply, and I'm afraid tonight must have been one such occasion, then Will sort of leaves the scene and those silenced parts of himself resurface as other personalities.
Charles	So Hal showed up because . . .
Wanda	Hal shows up when a group is not working. We were silent at the table and we were awkward – that's the sort of time.
Virginia	And Vladimir?
Wanda	That's the problem.

Tom   What is?

Wanda   Vladimir often shows up if I have had to trick Hal into
           leaving. Will will walk almost exactly a hundred yards
           north and when he sees that there are no cattle, he'll
           probably ask a few people if they've seen his herd, and
           sooner or later (and it's usually sooner) someone will
           laugh, and that brings him out of it.

Virginia   Couldn't we have laughed here at the table? Wouldn't that
           have turned him back into Will?

Wanda   No – Vladimir would have shown up instantly. It would
           have been extremely dangerous.

Tom   But he could come back in as someone else, not as
           Vladimir, is that right?

Wanda   There's a fifty-fifty chance.

Charles   What are the other possibles? Are his alters all American-
           inspired?

Wanda   He has watched a lot of American TV over the years.

Charles   Couldn't he just be content to be English?

Virginia   Oh God, Charles, what has that to do with anything?

Charles   Well, maybe Americans are multiples, and we would be all
           right if we didn't come into contact with them. It's
           possible we are all carrying this inside us, rather like a viral
           infection. If we stuck to being English . . .

Virginia   *(very anxious and impatient)* Oh Charles!

Wanda   You would all love Raoul.

Charles   Raoul?

Wanda   *(almost swooning)* He is so romantic. He will insist we all
           dance and pair off and . . . *(embarrassed)*

Virginia   And what?

Wanda	Well, you might not like him all that much, now that I come to think of it.
Virginia	Think of what?
Charles	What are you leaving out, Wanda?
Tom	Please, you must tell us.
Wanda	*(slowly)* He will insist that we all make love.
All (except Wanda)	What!
Wanda	Yes. We must dance, then we must make love.
Virginia	Well, for God's sake, what is one supposed to do then?
Wanda	You just have to go through with it.
Charles	Have to go through with it?
Wanda	It's not so bad.
Virginia	Wanda, for God's sake, it sounds horrible. What – dancing followed by enforced fucking! *(casts a withering glance at Charles)* Well, there goes your American theory, my dear. That's got to be from Brazilian TV!
Wanda	*(breaks down in tears again)* I'm so sorry.
Virginia	Oh, darling Wanda, forgive me. *(comforts her)*
Charles	So . . . what do we do?
Wanda	We go through with it and then it's over.
Tom	*(looking lasciviously at Clarissa, who bows her head)* How far do we go?
Wanda	We may have to go all the way to . . . you know . . . to . . .
Virginia	Actual intercourse?
Wanda	Yes . . . or at least until he has an orgasm, and then with luck Will should show up.

Charles	*(optimistic)* Oh. You mean we just have to pretend we're having sex until he comes and . . .
Wanda	No, that's extremely dangerous. If he thinks we're conning him then he'll flip into Vladimir and we will be . . .
Virginia	Out of position.
Wanda	That's right, we will be out of position and we will muck up our Miranda lines and we could be in serious danger. We . . . ah . . .
Virginia	What is it?
Wanda	We . . . may need to subdue him . . . violently.
Virginia	For God's sake.
Wanda	Ginny. All of you. *(looks around the group desperately)* Our lives may depend on our defending ourselves from Vladimir. If our Miranda does not work, and if for any reason he says 'you have been screwing with me', you only have a few seconds to subdue him. He then becomes murderous and he can . . . he . . .
Virginia	He can what?
Wanda	He can kill.
All (except Wanda)	What?
Wanda	He has killed.
Virginia	*(jumps up with a scream)* Oh help!
Tom	Ginny, quiet. No noise.
Wanda	You remember the 'Poker Party' slayings?
Charles	Five or six years ago, in the north of the city?
Wanda	Yes. It was Will.
Tom	But he wasn't caught.

Wanda   That's right. No one found out who it was.

Tom   How do you know it was Will?

Wanda   He TOLD me.

Tom   He told you?

Wanda   He hired Will as his lawyer, and Will told me.

Charles   Why didn't you go to the police?

Wanda   Because Will told me it was privileged information and
            that I must not tell. I was Will's legal clerk at the time and
            so I was bound to keep it to myself.

Tom   So why are you telling us this now?

Wanda   Because I resign. I've had enough. I can't take this any
            longer. It's too much. Just too much. He needs to be
            caught. People have died. And we must survive.

There is a loud knock at the front door.

Virginia   Oh my God, it's him. Quick – we must all go and sit
            down.

*They all leave the dinner table and rush to the chairs, trying to look
relaxed.*

Act four

Scene one

The characters are in exactly the same positions as at the end of the last act. It is as if they have again been frozen in time. All are seated and the banging on the door continues. Finally Charles gets up, walks down the passageway towards the front door, and returns, walking rather quickly ahead of Will.

Will	Phew! What a walk! *(the group is staring at him, looking wan)*
Wanda	Will, I . . .
Will	Will what?
Virginia	I think she means, will you like to sit down?
Will	What – sit, when you can dance?
All (except Will)	Raoul!
Wanda	Oh, thank God.
Virginia	We are so relieved.
Charles	We were afraid you could be . . .
Virginia	Quiet, Charles!
Tom	Music, Raoul?

They rise from their chairs, almost in unison, and Charles goes over to the stereo and puts on a Piazzola tango.

Will   Let's dance, let's get it on. Music! Music! Music!

Will turns down the lights, goes over and grabs Virginia and draws her right against him, grinding into her. They 'dance' a type of tango. It is clear from the beginning that his idea of dancing is thinly concealed simulated intercourse; Virginia is alternately horrified and caught up in his movements. They dance alone for about 45 seconds, with the rest of the group gawping, arms dropped, looking helpless.

         What's the matter with you all?

Still dancing but now looking at the others, Will whirls Virginia around, moving her to each member of the group in turn.

            Come on, find a partner, find a partner! This is good for
            us! We have to get into this. We have to get out of
            ourselves, lose ourselves. This is the only way. It's crazy to
            be sitting around when you can dance. Right? Right?
            *(peering in each person's face as he dances with Virginia from
            one to the next)* Am I right? Right, yes? All right! All right.

Virginia begins to swoon. It is not clear whether she is terrified or is beginning to respond to Will's sexuality, but soon we hear sonic images of a woman becoming increasingly sexually excited – a long low moan, another moan, and she begins to get into it. Tom grabs Clarissa in a primitive and compelling way and she begins to take off his shirt; for about 30 seconds they dance and grab at each other. Charles gets hold of Wanda, fearful of being left outside the action and vulnerable to Will's state of mind. Wanda, however, keeps him at arm's length. Her gaze is constantly directed towards Virginia and Will, and it is clear that she is distressed by their increasing sexual activity. As their dance intensifies, Virginia caresses Will, opens her legs to him, puts her foot on his shoulder, and takes part in a choreography of wanton desire. Wanda pushes Charles away but he grabs her back in what becomes a tug of war between the two; Wanda wants to escape but Charles hangs on for dear life. Clarissa climbs onto a chair and pulls Tom's head into her groin while she weaves her body over and around him.

Wanda suddenly slaps Charles and pushes him violently to the side.

Wanda   *(yells)* Vladimir Smirnoff, the authorities have something
               to say to you.

*Tom and Clarissa jump to attention and hold hands. Charles stands alone,
looking dumbstruck. Virginia is still dancing with Will. Wanda goes over to
the stereo and turns off the music.*

               I said: Vladimir Smirnoff, the authorities have something
               to say to you.

Will   What the hell?

Charles   Are we?

Tom   Wanda, are you sure . . . now?

Wanda   Our lives depend on it!

All (except   You have the right to remain silent. You have the right to
Will)   an attorney. Anything you say now can and will be used
               against you in a court of law. Do you understand what has
               been said to you?

Will   What?

Wanda   Again!

All (except   You have the right to remain silent. You have the right to
Will)   an attorney. Anything you say now can and will be used
               against you in a court of law. Do you understand what has
               been said to you?

*The group is sobering up. Will pushes Virginia to the ground, where she lies
half moaning, half recomposing herself. He walks to the centre of the room.
All are now silent. Will walks up to each person and peers into their eyes,
saying nothing. They are terrified but try to remain composed.*

Will   *(calmly, icily)* What did you say?

Wanda   You heard what we said.

Will   *(to Charles)* What did you say?

Charles	I . . . I . . . You want me to repeat it?
Will	I want you to tell me what you just said.
Charles	Did, did it work?
Will	Work?
Charles	Yes, I mean . . . to whom am I speaking, please?
Wanda	Don't, Charles, be careful . . .
Will	To whom are you speaking?
Charles	To who?
Will	Who or whom, who gives a shit. For whom do you take me?
Charles	Raoul?
Will	Raoul?
Charles	Raoul?
Will	Who the fuck is Raoul?
Charles	An idea, an idea in my mind, I'm sure. Just an idea. The . . . A sort of wrong idea?
Will	*(walking over to Tom)* Young man, whom do you take me for?
Tom	I wouldn't want to say.
Will	You wouldn't want to say?
Tom	No, Sir.
Will	Sir?
Tom	Yes, Sir.
Will	You wouldn't want to say, Sir, and you don't know why?
Tom	I . . . *(Clarissa grabs Tom protectively and he accepts her protection)*

Will   Okay. Okay. You need her. *(walks calmly over to Virginia, who is still on the floor)* Here, let me help you. Take my hand.

Virginia looks up at him, tearful. She takes his hand and their eyes meet in an intense gaze. He speaks in a lowered voice.

              Who do you think I am?

Virginia   I . . . I . . .

She looks at him, trying to find words, but then seems embarrassed. It is clear from this point forward that Virginia is not entirely acting and has been genuinely sexually dislodged by Will. She will recite her lines but often without looking at the person to whom she is speaking, and in subtle ways members of the cast will note this change and swap nervous glances.

Wanda   *(out of role, whispers to Virginia)* 'I don't think I know who you are.'

Will   Who am I to you? Who am I to all of you? *(looking around the group)* I've been away, what, fifteen minutes, and come back to a group of people who don't know who I am. Tell me, who do YOU think I am?

Will looks again at Virginia, who now disengages from him. She walks around the room, absent-mindedly picks up an ashtray, then looks up at the ceiling, sighs, puts the ashtray down on the dinner table, and puts both hands in her crotch.

Virginia   You are, uh . . .

Wanda moves closer to her and again feeds Virginia her lines.

Wanda   'You're a man. A man of amazing talent and presence. A man who has so many dimensions and strengths and possesses the power to displace sense. You seem to render us senseless.'

Virginia   *(repeats the lines, but without feeling)* You're a man of amazing talent and presence. A man who has so many

157

dimensions and strengths and possesses the power to displace sense.

From this point forward, each time Virginia is meant to speak, she draws a blank and the audience hears the off-stage prompter whispering her lines.

Will   I leave and return, I go and come back, and find this reception. You feel I have displaced you? Virginia, you tell me, who is out of place here? Who ARE YOU? I mean it, who are you to call into question my place? And what was that – that chant you all . . . What was that, Virginia?

Virginia   *(blank, then we hear the lines whispered to her)* Will. I mean Raoul, *(whispering)* we were calling you. *(whispering)* We were making a call to you. *(whispering)* We were making a call to see whether you were . . . *(whispering)* the person you appeared to be or were someone else, someone who could take your place.

The others now appear awkward. They look anxiously back and forth at one another, they walk about, occasionally bang into one another and apologise, clearly losing the sense of ensemble. Will's tone has completely changed and he is no longer fully in the role, as he realises that Virginia cannot remember her lines.

Will   Okay, I see what's happened. It's clear. But you, Virginia, must tell me. *(it is clear to the cast that Will has enunciated Virginia's name very deliberately, to try to get the actress back into role)* In your own words, you tell me what has happened.

Virginia   *(looking at various members of the cast and finally out to the audience)* I am so sorry. So sorry. I feel so stupid. What a horrible situation. I don't know what's happened. I'm just a blank. It's everyone's nightmare. You'll have to continue without me. I . . .

Virginia runs off-stage. The other members of the cast look gobsmacked. Someone off-stage yells 'curtain' and the stage goes dark. It is clear that no one has actually left the stage, as we can hear the actors moving about and whispering to one another. After a minute or so, the lights come back on.

Scene two

All are now seated and motionless as if waiting to be brought to life, except for Charles, who stands up and walks to centre stage front and directly addresses the audience.

Charles   I do apologise to you on behalf of my wife, who is not herself at the moment and who I hope will return. The dinner party must go on, I'm sure you will all agree, and as necessity is the mother of invention, we shall fill in for Ginny as we go along and just get to the end of the party so we can then all go home. Thank you for your forbearance.

Charles returns to his seat. The cast members seem to count to five and then come to life.

Will   So, Wanda, do you tell them or do I?

Charles   I don't know what you mean.

Will   Well, apologies are going around on behalf of wives, it would seem, so now I make one of my own. Wanda, my lovely wife, is a Munchausen's by proxy. That means she invents illnesses to earn her special time with the authorities, or anyone who will sympathise. She tells people that I am a multiple personality and she invents strategies for them to deal with me.

Wanda   Don't believe what he's saying. He's turning into Vladimir. Be careful. We must stop this.

Will   And who is Vladimir, my dear?

Wanda   You should know him, Will, but you don't, do you? I mean, you just piss off and become whoever you like, and leave the rest to us. We're always cleaning up your mess, aren't we? We're always left with the detritus of your characters. We are the clean-up crew, the bin men, left in the wake of your appalling narcissism.

Will	And just how has that manifested itself tonight, my love?
Wanda	*(stands)* Oh, don't give us this crap. You left. You left us. Didn't you? *(looks around the room for support)* You turned into bloody John Wayne with your stupid cattle and your need for a walk. You just wanted to bail out of the room because you'd had enough. But would you own up to this? Of course not. That would mean your assuming agency for your existence, rather than subdividing your huge personality into its idiotic parts.
Charles	Wanda, I'm not sure we want to upset him. Maybe Will is just into Americana . . . ? Er, with a dash of Brazil, now and then?
Wanda	Oh, I'm tired of the whole thing. I frankly don't care if he kills us all. Look what happened to poor Virginia. Can't remember her blessed lines. Completely blank. Taken to her bed, I bet.
Will	Taken ill. Taken ill. Your preferred course of events. *(looks at Charles, then Tom)* Have you been taken in by this? Do you . . . You don't believe what she's been telling you, do you?
Tom	Er, Will, it's . . . Do we have to get into this?
Will	I'm afraid we do. You have read me my rights. Well, I'm a lawyer, now hired to represent myself and I am deposing you. *(takes out a notepad)* You understand that you are all under oath to tell the truth, the whole truth, and nothing but the truth, so help you God? *(they all nod and Wanda sits down, fuming)*
Wanda	Well, he's done this before, but I haven't seen it in a long time.
Clarissa	What does it mean? Are we safe?
Wanda	As long as he becomes his own lawyer, you are okay. I'm tired of predicting him, however. I have no idea where this

	is going. We could survive or, frankly, he could decide to kill the lot of us.
Will	What did you say? *(rushes over to Wanda and looms threateningly)*
Wanda	I said you could decide to kill the lot of us, didn't I?
Will	What are you talking about?
Wanda	Well, big shot lawyer, why don't you interview Vladimir Smirnoff and find out for yourself!
Charles	Wanda, no! Let's not go there.
Tom	Please, Wanda. The whole of America could be over here any moment!
Clarissa	I don't want to die. I've just found my love. *(she and Tom cuddle)*
Wanda	I'm tired of it all. Can't you see? Can't you see how exhausting and unending this is? How I've no idea who this man is? I've lived with him for, what, twenty-five years, and I still have no idea who he is. I mean, he could REALLY be Raoul, couldn't he? I mean, you all saw that, didn't you? Good old lawyerly Will, old straightforward, calm-talking Will. What are we to believe: Will or Raoul? And if Vladimir the psychotic shithead ever does show up, well, what will any of us believe after that?
Will	It was my John Wayne act, wasn't it?
Charles	Sorry?
Will	It was my John Wayne act at the table, you know, when I said I had to go out and collect the little dogies, my cattle.
Charles	You remember that?
Will	Christ, man – of course I remember it! I invented it. I just made it up.

Charles	But why?
Tom	Why do something like that?
Will	Why? Young man, you of all people should ask! But again, that shows it was the right thing to do. You and this beautiful woman of yours were so into one another you were freaking us out, so I decided to break the tension and get us to somewhere else. And quite frankly I needed a break. It was a bit heavy, you have to agree.
Wanda	Always pissing off, leaving the remains to the rest of us.
Charles	You mean, you ACTED like John Wayne. You made that all up in order to get out of the situation?
Will	Of course.
Charles	And what about this Raoul stuff on your return?
Will	What Raoul stuff?
Charles	You know, when you vamped Virginia after I turned on the music and we all practically fucked one another, except . . .
Will	Except for you and Wanda, right?
Wanda	He is disgusting.
Will	You got stuck with Wanda, didn't you, poor chap!
Charles	I was perfectly content with that.
Wanda	Indeed he was. He was safe with me. Safe.
Charles	You were playing a part, weren't you, Will?
Will	No, that was me. I'm fed up with her sickliness. She can't dance. We don't fuck any more. Her back hurts, or she's dying of cancer – oh, I'm sorry Tom – but she's always ill, something is always wrong, so when I came into the room and saw all of you looking like death had come over you, I just said to myself 'fuck it', called for the music, turned

down the lights, and yes, I did grab Virginia, because she is or was the life of the party. And it got us going.

Tom   Will, we thought you were going to kill us. We thought that if we didn't go along with you, if we didn't pretend you were Raoul then you might turn into Vladimir and …

Clarissa starts to button up her blouse. Will is writing everything down.

Charles Will, why are you writing?

Will   It's important to get this down.

Charles To what end?

Will   Well, a moment ago the group believed that I was a criminal, made a citizen's arrest and read me my rights, so I need legal defence and this will be my best opportunity.

Tom   But it was just a mistake.

Wanda   It's no mistake, you're just falling into the trap. Vladimir is just around the corner. You will have to think of how to defend yourselves. It's not up to me now – you're on your own.

Charles *(backing up a bit)* Will?

Will   It depends on whom you choose to believe, Charles. You can believe Wanda's narrative or mine.

Charles But there is an important difference.

Tom   If Wanda is right, we could be killed. If you are right, we have just been terrorised but there is no actual danger.

Wanda   These are not narratives.

Will   Oh yes they are, dear. And both are terrorising.

Wanda   One is true, one is false.

Will   Yes indeed.

Tom	But they are both so plausible. I mean, short of a polygraph test, it's impossible for us to know which one of the two of you is . . .
Will	Lying?
Tom	Well . . .
Will	It's okay, Tom. I take no offence. You're right. They are narratives but when one narrative is true and the other is false, it sort of nullifies narrative theory, don't you think?
Tom	Yeah, if you're actually, you know . . .
Charles	Between two ideas, one of which could kill you.
Clarissa	I don't want to die, Tom, I feel I've just been born.

A strange woman in Virginia's clothing enters the room and sits down, looking anxious but trying to fit in.

Charles	Oh, hi!
Understudy	Hi.
Tom	Who is . . .
Charles	*(brightly)* Look, it's Virginia, she's feeling better.
Understudy	Yes, I'm sorry. I feel better now.
Wanda	Well, good.
Will	Yes, good to have you back.
Understudy	So, where are we?
Charles	We don't know who or what to believe. If we believe Wanda, then Will is a multiple personality with one part of him – Vladimir – capable of killing all of us. If we believe Will, then Wanda is a Munchausen's by proxy and she's just making all of this up in order to gain our sympathy and earn her tickets to the hospital.

Understudy Well, Will – or whoever you are – I understand you really did me in the dance! *(laughs nervously, as the others look completely dumbstruck)*

Will Well, it was something.

Understudy I feel as if I've missed out.

Will Not really.

Understudy No, really, I feel as if I've missed out on something, as if I had amnesia.

Clarissa Like me?

Understudy Like you, yes, like you. It was as if I wasn't here. Show me . . . You . . . *(points to Clarissa)* you show me how he did it.

Tom walks over to the stereo and puts on another haunting Piazzola tune, but Will stays put this time. Tom stands in and begins dancing with Clarissa, and the two of them once again become hypnotic.

Wanda *(yelling over the music)* I don't like where this is going!

Charles Where is that?

Wanda Into something very uncertain.

Charles Because of the dancing?

Wanda Because of the chemistry.

Charles The chemistry?

Wanda You can't feel it?

Charles I don't know.

Wanda Get out of your head, Charles, and try to feel the chemistry. Something is happening, something combustible. *(Will starts to pace up and down the room)* He's pacing.

Charles What does that mean?

Wanda	It's a bad sign, a bad sign.
Charles	A sign of what?
Wanda	Of violent change. Of violent transformation.
Charles	What can we do?
Wanda	Turn off the music. Turn off the music!
Charles	I . . .

Charles walks over to the stereo and turns off the music. The sudden silence freezes Tom and Clarissa, who put their hands in front of their genitals, like Adam and Eve caught out by God. They cower slightly and then hold each other.

Will	*(in a booming, resonant voice)* Evil! Evil is present.
Understudy	How do you mean? What evil? Where?
Will	Evil is present, you can feel it. It is in the air. It is moving about amongst us. Some dark thing is moving about in our midst. It has us in its grip.
Wanda	You see!
Charles	Is it Vladimir?

There is a loud knock at the front door.

Robert	*(yelling, off-stage)* Open up, open up!

Charles exits and reappears leading Robert, a young man, into the room. Upon seeing him, Clarissa cowers and hides behind Tom. Robert looks confused, flustered and impatient.

Charles	Look who I found!
Robert	What the hell is going on here?
Will	Jesus. Aren't you the guy who was in the street beating up on Clarissa . . . ? But it's Robert! You're Robert! My God, you've changed. Unrecognisable. Is it the haircut?

Robert   Yeah, whatever. Look . . .

Understudy *(said without meaning)* We're so glad to see you, son.

Robert   Who the fuck . . .

Charles   It's Virginia, your mother!

Looking a bit strained, Charles glances at the others, who also seem thunderstruck. He raises his hands in a gesture to Robert, as if to say 'Come on . . . you know.'

Robert   They could have bloody well told me . . .

Charles   Late, late as usual, I guess. Oh well, when you're late you miss out on what's happened before, but on the other hand . . .

Will   Things are more challenging, slightly more interesting.

Robert   Whatever. Look, I . . . *(sees Clarissa hiding behind Tom)* Shit, I knew it. I just knew it. What the hell are you doing here?

Clarissa   It's him. It's the man who was beating me in the street. Save me! *(Tom puts his hand up)*

Tom   Back off, Robert.

Robert   Tom, you poor bugger. Have you been taken in by this?

Tom   By what? And be careful what you say and how you say it.

Robert   Whatever she calls herself, that person cowering behind you is a phoney – a complete con-woman.

Tom   Be careful.

Charles   Son, I don't know if . . .

Robert   You idiot. You stupid idiot. You can't recognise your own daughter?

Understudy What?

Robert   Well, YOU I understand. What would you know, anyway, whoever you are?

Charles   Don't talk to your mother like that.

Robert   *(snorts with contemptuous laughter)* Yeah, right!

Suddenly the original Virginia walks back into the room, in something of a daze. The cast are stunned but Will walks over to her right away and holds her hand. The understudy stamps her foot in frustration and looks out into the lights for some help, but none is forthcoming.

Virginia   Oh – hi, everyone. Sorry. Sorry. Sorry. I'm all right now. Can go on. No longer blank. *(sees her understudy)* Oh . . . Oh, hello, sweetie. I'm so glad to see you. It's like having another me here, isn't it?

Robert   Right – a bloody clone. Look, MOTHER, *(staring very hard at Virginia)* will you just look at who's in the fucking room.

Virginia   Who, darling?

Robert   What, you too?

Virginia   What, darling?

Robert   Are you kidding? I can't believe it! I mean, living with Einstein here . . .

Charles   It's Eysenck, actually.

Robert   Right, living with Eysenck can't be all that intellectually stimulating, but surely you can recognise your own flesh and blood.

Virginia   Of course I, we, do. *(looks at the understudy)* Don't we?

Understudy *(moving quickly to stand next to Virginia)* Yes, of course we do.

Robert   *(laughing)* What – a royal 'we'! A royal fucking 'we'. So you recognise your daughter, do you? So, then, where is she? *(both women look at Will)*

Will	What are you looking at me for?
Virginia	We know . . . um . . . that you have this amazing power of . . . um . . .
Will	Oh come off it, you don't think . . . ?
Wanda	No, forget it, he's never been a woman. God, if I could only get him to be a woman . . .
Robert	*(looking at Clarissa)* Your time's up, babe. It's all over.
Virginia	Robert, I don't think you should talk to our guest like that.
Robert	Go on – look at her. Go on. Walk up to her. Get a good look. *(Virginia and the understudy go up to Clarissa and study her)* Well, smell her, then. *(they both sniff)*
Virginia	Rebecca?
Clarissa	I'm Clarissa.
Virginia	*(her voice is raised in alarm)* Becky, love? Becky?
Clarissa	That's not who I am.
Virginia	*(screaming at her, she yanks off the red wig to reveal blonde hair)* Becky!
Tom	No! No! No! *(deeply anguished, he lunges at Virginia, grabs the wig, buries his face in it and starts sobbing)* Clarissa, come back. Come back.
Clarissa	I'm here, darling. I'm here. *(Tom appears not to hear her and continues to hold on to the wig)*
Virginia	*(to Clarissa)* Where have you been all these years?
Clarissa	I don't know what you mean.
Charles	Rebecca, you left us.
Clarissa	I don't know who you are.

| Charles | This is your mother, who gave birth to you. |

| Virginia | Out of MY body! Out of my body. My body . . . |

Virginia breaks down, sobbing. She sits down in a side chair and Tom walks over and stands next to her. Virginia leans into Tom and Tom puts his hand on her shoulder.

| Robert | *(to Clarissa)* Look at the rubbish you've brought on yourself and on these poor buggers. |

| Will | What are you talking about, Bob? |

| Robert | It's not 'Bob', Will, it never was. It's Robert, just as you are not 'Willy', that idiot should not be 'Charlie', and you . . . *(looks at Wanda)* Oh fuck, you should never have been named 'Wanda'. |

| Wanda | Whatever do . . . |

| Robert | Well, what sort of a name is that? Wands. Wands waving. Who could ever live with 'Wanda'? |

| Will | Well, I can tell you it's hell. |

| Robert | I don't mean that – I mean, how could she ever live with a name like that? Parents curse us with our so-called 'proper' names. *(looks back at Clarissa)* But maybe you are a 'Becky', a beck, a hussy who abandons her name and picks anything she fancies in order to get what she wants. What about it, Beck? *(imitates a chicken pecking at the ground)* Beck, Beck, Beck. |

Tom has now wiped his eyes and he helps Virginia to her feet. He takes the wig and puts it back on Clarissa's head; grateful, she arranges it properly.

| Tom | She is my Clarissa and I love her. |

| Robert | She is my sister. She has conned you. She has always had a thing for you, and when she heard your wife was ill she found out everything she could about it. When your wife checked into the Medici, this con-artist *(points at Clarissa)* |

stepped in front of a fucking bus so she could get admitted, faked a coma, and then feigned amnesia. Somehow she got herself moved into the room next to your wife so she could overhear you talking. She was studying your wife – every detail. When she heard you were coming tonight, she dressed up like Antonia and came right over here. I KNOW this is what she did. I'm her brother. I had to live with her for years! Too much crazy shit has happened in this house.

Charles   Robert, maybe she isn't doing any harm.

Robert   Oh God, Dad, please!

Clarissa   It isn't like Robert says. It isn't like that. *(everyone looks at her in silence)* I loved Tom. I felt something awaken deep inside me as I got to know him over the years. I dreamed of him, every night. I felt we were meant for each other. I was thinking of him when I stepped in front of the bus – not because I wanted to be injured, but because I was distracted.

Understudy   DID you fake the coma?

Clarissa   How would I know?

Understudy   Because you would have been awake and known what you were doing. You would remember that, wouldn't you?

Clarissa   But I often don't know, even when I am awake, what is real. I have to believe I was asleep, even though the creep-brother here thinks I'm lying. But he always thought I was lying. He never trusted me.

Will   And your identification with his wife?

Clarissa   I always looked like her, but none of you noticed. I think Tom did, but I was younger then and I wasn't sure that he saw it.

Will   But the red hair?

Clarissa	When I first woke up in hospital, Dr Sprecht asked if I wanted anything special and I said I wanted to have red hair. I didn't know at the time why I was asking this.
Charles	Maybe we can look on the good side of this?
Robert	Right, where is that?
Charles	Well, it's in the mind, isn't it? It's what we think that matters. If Rebecca wants to be Antonia . . .
Clarissa	Clarissa.
Charles	If Rebecca wants to be Clarissa, then if she thinks she is Clarissa, for all intents and purposes she is Clarissa. I mean, if that idea proves transformational, then . . .
Robert	Oh, so this is your pathetic cognitive therapy.
Charles	Well, hold on. Hold on. Ideas change the world. We can change the world by changing ideas, and if Tom sees Antonia in Clarissa then he is cured of his loss.
Tom	She knows me.
Clarissa	I know.
Charles	Right – you think so, and that's what's important.
Wanda	And if Roboman here *(looks at Will)* thinks he's a serial killer from the Russian steppes, we're just supposed to go along with his way of thinking, is that it?
Charles	No, we are supposed to change his mind. We are supposed to show him that he has the wrong idea about himself.
Wanda	And exactly how do we do that?
Charles	Well, we uh . . . we uh . . . *(holds his nose between his fingers)* We have to reason with him to show him how being Vlad is not good for him, how it is counterproductive, and how thinking of being someone else is a much better idea.

Will	Charles, don't fall for Wanda's bullshit.
Charles	Well, Will, just for discussion's sake, let's imagine for a moment that Wanda needs to have these theories about you. She needs to think this way.
Will	What good does that do me?
Charles	Well, that's hard to tell, although no one would say having the two of you around wasn't interesting.
Wanda	Try the fourteen of us.
Charles	Yeah! *(he laughs and Will turns his back on him)* No, Will, I mean, if that's what Wanda needs to think, or what she thinks she needs to think, then all you have to do is help her change her mind.
Will	*(whirls around, irritated)* How the hell do I do that? What would you do if you were married to someone who told friends and colleagues – even strangers – that you were a multiple personality?
Robert	My father hasn't even got one personality. *(angry, walking around the room)* My mother's out to lunch, and my sister's a scheming psychopath.
Charles	Well, I'm sorry that you think this way, Robert.
Robert	I don't 'think this way', Dad, this is the way it is.
Charles	You're printing your edition of the paper, son.
Robert	No, I'm telling the truth! I mean, does anyone here know what the fuck that is? *(looking from face to face and talking to each in turn)* You've lost your wife – a complete clone walks into the room and you don't even ask any questions. Don't you care whether you're being conned or not? *(to Wanda)* Don't you want to know which one of the two of you is fucked? Who's the mad one? Does anyone here know which one of these two is crazy? *(to Charles again)* And as for you, Karnac. Do you give a damn about the

truth, or only what people think is true? You serve people warmed-up Dale Carnegie – 'The Power of Positive Thinking'. It's only in the mind, and all we have to do is change our ideas. Doesn't it bother you that your so-called cognitive therapy is just one huge con?

Charles   It's science, son.

Robert   Bullshit. It's marketing. You psychologists don't know what the fuck you're doing, so you come up with some nifty words, a few clichés, and band together in your thousands chanting 'cognitive therapy', 'cognitive therapy', 'cognitive therapy', so that it becomes a kind of bonding litany – a new Song of Songs.

Charles   No, son, that's an idea in your head. It's not reality.

Robert   You just harvest the history of ideas by substituting 'cognitive' for everything else, so now we have a cognitive theory of dreams, of symptoms, of sexual relations. And all you do is repeat the same crap: that it's just ideas in our heads and all we have to do is change them. You're like some branch of McDonald's – just pop in for a bit of a head feed, and bad ideas leave and good ideas come in. It's fast-food psychology.

Charles   *(looking rather helpless)* Well, son, at least it gets you thinking and feeling something passionately.

Virginia   I think I'm feeling unwell.

Virginia sits down suddenly. The others give her quick, nervous glances. It is clear the ensemble is slightly thrown off, but they continue as if nothing has happened.

Wanda   Who isn't?

Virginia   REALLY, I'm not.

Wanda   Yes, but . . . you know . . . You as VIRGINIA, or you . . .

Understudy   *(bright and cheery, trying to reassure the cast she can step back into the role)* I'm feeling all right.

Wanda   Yes, I know YOU are, dear.

Virginia   I think . . . it's very strange, all of this, don't you think?

She is speaking to the entire group but no one knows what to make of it; they do not know whether she is still in her role as Virginia, and ad-libbing, or whether she has come out of role.

I mean, it's very strange to have a character, don't you think?

Will   To be IN character, or to . . . ?

Virginia   To be a character. It is just all so PECULIAR. *(starts to laugh hysterically)* I mean, it's all so stupid to be who we are, don't you think? Don't you think it's hilarious to wake up every morning to the same face in the mirror, to the same name, to have to be known by the same name, and to have the same habits? It's not as if we choose this, do we? Except when we act, of course. Now, acting . . .

The other cast members are stupefied. They hold out their hands, or put their fingers to their to lips to try to stop her.

Will   *(jumping in nervously)* . . . which one could do if one wanted to, but which we are not doing now, are we?

Virginia   I don't know what on earth you mean. I just think to be anyone is weird. It just seems so presumptuous.

Wanda   Presumptuous?

Virginia   Yes. How do I know who I am? On what basis do I proceed to inhabit myself? I mean, when we wake up in the morning, don't we have to remind ourselves who we are?

Clarissa   Because in our dreams we have been other people?

Clarissa is not acting now – she becomes genuinely caught up in Virginia's questioning. As she does so, other members of the cast appear more relaxed, as if the production is over and they can now talk freely.

Virginia   We have been so MANY other people and in so many different places. It's so much more interesting than boring old REALITY, and all the predictable things of life. How do we get ourselves into this mess? Because we never question our character. We never say to ourselves: 'Hey, wait a minute. This is my life. I only live once. Do I agree to this name? Do I agree to "Veronica"?'

Charles   *(half-heartedly trying to retrieve the situation)* Virginia.

Virginia   Whatever. Veronica, Virginia. Do I agree to this? Maybe I don't. Maybe I don't agree at all. Maybe I hate this name. Maybe I shall be someone else today. But . . . that's boring too. It's just as boring to be someone else, because that's just being forced into another mould.

Robert   I've been away too long. At last you're making sense. Go for it. I agree – we are trapped in our characters. We should all just say 'fuck it, I can't take it any more' and we should throw away our driving licences, our passports, our chequebooks, and get rid of our names.

Clarissa   We could be anyone we wanted to be.

Robert   *(suddenly uncertain)* Yeah, well . . . it's liberation for good or for bad. It depends.

Robert still seems very much in role, and his strident aggression towards Clarissa brings the rest of the cast back into character.

Charles   It depends on what ideas we have in our minds.

Robert   That's bullshit. You can't micro-manage what Mum's talking about. *(embarrassed)* 'Mum' . . . think of that word. It's an embarrassing word. Why should I have to talk to you like that? Why do we get stuck with 'Mum' and 'Dad', like fucking nincompoops?

Charles	Okay, change our names and see if that doesn't change your mind.
Robert	Okay, how about 'Asshole' for you! *(elated, laughing)* What about 'Asshole'? *(arms pumping up and down, increasingly enthusiastic)* If that makes me feel better, if that means I can bear you because I get to say this, then what?
Charles	If it makes you feel better, so be it.
Robert	Okay, Asshole. I can't tell you how much better it's making me feel. You try it, Will.
Will	Try . . . what?
Robert	Go ahead, give it a go.
Will	How?
Wanda	He wants to know what name you could have for me that would be liberating, you know, like he feels liberated now that he can call Charles 'Asshole'.
Will	You look like a fucking MISSIONARY WORKER.
All (except Will and Wanda)	Wheeew!
Wanda	What?
Will	You meddling old fart. You dress like, think like, talk like, and act like, a suffocating, self-righteous missionary worker.
Wanda	Oh, really? That's what you call me?
Will	Absolutely.
Wanda	That makes you feel better?
Will	It makes me feel great! *(beaming, he goes over to Robert and they high-five)*

Wanda	Okay, fair's fair. Then maybe you can at last benefit from my mission, you ill-fitted wanker.
Charles	Is there some other name you might use that would, uh, would make you feel liberated?
Wanda	There certainly is! *(she walks up to Will, stands a few inches from his face and speaks very slowly)* Penis Drop.
Charles	What was that? It was hard to hear.
Wanda	I said: *(yelling)* Penis Drop! You may be called Will, and that may lead lots of the innocent to think of you as a force of will or of willy, but I know you for what you are, you impotent clown. You are Penis Drop. That's your name.

She puts her hands between her legs, as if she is going to wet herself, and starts laughing. Eventually she falls backwards into a chair, laughing and chanting the name. Will becomes rigid and motionless, standing like a soldier being dressed down by a superior officer.

Penis Drop. Penis Drop. Penis Drop.

Will suddenly brings his right hand to cover his mouth, as if to suppress a violent remark, but otherwise he still remains quite motionless.

Tom	I think maybe we should stop this.
Charles	You can see, though, how liberated people feel. Just a change of name is liberating. I mean, I'm 'Asshole' now and I feel pretty good about it.
Robert	That's because you are an Asshole!
Charles	*(laughing weakly)* I guess that's so. If you think so.
Robert	I get to call you that, right?
Charles	What do you mean?
Robert	I mean, in the street, at the newsagent's, or the pub, or the match, I get to say 'Hey, hello there, Asshole' and you'll accept this. You'll acknowledge this as your name?

Charles	But I never see you! You haven't spent time with me in years.
Robert	Yeah, but I would now.
Understudy	Oh, that's nice, isn't it?
Charles	Well, if it means we can hang out.
Robert	Oh, it does. I would love it.
Charles	It's just a name.
Robert	No, Asshole, it's an idea. It's the right idea and your own theory supports that.
Will	*(now drops his right hand, and relaxes as if he has suddenly been brought out of his own state of shock and rage)* But Robert, it could hurt his feelings.
Robert	No, impossible.
Tom	I wouldn't want to be called 'Asshole'.
Robert	Because, Tom, you aren't an Asshole. But he is. And he knows it. He has to accept this name, as it identifies him.
Virginia	I'm not feeling well. Really.

The group is momentarily paralysed again.

	I think I need something.
Charles	What do you need?
Virginia	I think I need . . . The room is feeling funny to me.
Charles	I think we need some water, right now.

They all look around for water; Wanda pours a glass from a decanter on the table and gives it to Virginia. She drinks it slowly, as though it were nectar. The cast is still fixated on Virginia, worried about what she will say.

Virginia	Well, I think we've all had about enough, don't you?

All (except Virginia)	Enough?
Virginia	Yes, I think we've all had just about enough of this. Does anyone know what time it is?
Tom	Um, what kind of time, Virginia?
Virginia	The time, Tom. What does 'the time' mean, if not The Time?
Charles	Well, it's relative, dear. I mean, the time in New York is different from the time in, say, London.
Virginia	I mean the time here, the time now.
Charles	The real time?
Tom	It's, ah . . .

Tom reads off the real time at that moment. The other members of the cast look at their watches and agree.

Virginia	So, how much more time is there before we have to go?
Tom	You mean, before we die?
Virginia	Well, if that's what it means to you, okay.
Charles	Well, I don't know how we know. That's something cognitive therapy is working on, but we . . .
Robert	Oh come on, Asshole, don't tell me you guys are coming up with an idea that will morph death into something else.
Charles	We think there is a real possibility of . . .
Tom	Of what, Charles?
Charles	Of re-thinking it.
Wanda	What will that do?
Charles	It will change death in our minds, so then if we can think of it differently, we should be able to influence it.

Robert   Oh, I get it. So if we think death is really entrance into heaven, then we don't have to fear the end of our life – we are just beginning the wonderful afterlife, is that it, Asshole?

Charles   I wouldn't put it that crudely, but we do think that Christianity may have been the first true cognitive therapy. Mind working over matter.

Clarissa   So, father, you believe in the Resurrection?

Charles   I do, yes.

Clarissa   Was that mind over matter?

Charles   Jesus believed he was the son of God and his belief was so powerful that he was transubstantiated. I think we can be capable of that in time, but it may take several generations before we can achieve it.

Clarissa   So – and I'm sorry, Tom – so my love of Tom and my study of him, which has helped me to become Clarissa, which is who I really am now – and, I hope, for ever – *(looks at Tom and squeezes his hand)* is some early form of trans . . . trans . . .

Robert   Transubstantiation, idiot. But you are proof of how future generations could fuck this up.

Clarissa   You terrorist!

All (except What?
Clarissa)

Clarissa   Go on, Robert, tell them who you really are!

Robert   *(looks confused and furious)* Fuck off, Rebecca.

Will   What does she mean, 'terrorist'?

Clarissa   Go on – tell them, Robert, you're one for telling the truth. Why 'terrorist'?

Charles	Son?
Robert	Shut up, Asshole.
Clarissa	He's a member of a terrorist group and he'll kill me if I say which one.

Robert suddenly pulls a Berenger from his back pocket and points it at each person in turn.

Charles	Oh no – I knew we should have called the police.
Virginia	Are we going to be killed?
Wanda	This is serious. This is very serious. Is it loaded?
Robert	What do you think this is, play? Is this playtime? You think I'd show up here and hang out in this situation for the fun of it? *(takes a hat from his other back pocket and throws it at Charles)* Okay, Asshole. Put your wallet in there. All of you – you too, Penis Drop. All of you. *(they all reach for wallets or purses)* You're going to make a small contribution to the cause.

Robert reaches into his left front pocket and pulls out a number of pieces of paper, which he hands out, one to each member of the cast.

Okay, these are your new identities. You go down to the bank, register in your new names, get your new credit cards, all that shit, and you keep putting money in the account, or one of the brothers comes back and tops one of you.

Tom	What is this for?
Robert	It's a fundraiser. I'm your local branch. I raise funds for my group. *(to Clarissa)* You want me to call you 'Clarissa'? *(Clarissa nods)* Not your real name? *(she nods again)* Then you keep the fuck quiet about this. All of you. All the shit you've laid on each other this evening, all that shit is on record.

Will	What kind of record?
Robert	Yeah, well, you figure that out, genius. You figure that out. And when you do, you keep the fuck quiet. Right?
Will	Right. Anyway, if you hire me, it's all privileged.
Robert	What's your fee?
Will	Well, usually it's £400 an hour.
Robert	That's fucking highway robbery.
Will	I can offer a discount.
Robert	You take £20. *(throws the money at Will and moves towards the passageway stage right)* Well, it's been nice seeing you all again. And remember – I'm keeping my eye on you.
Virginia	On who?
Robert	On whoever the fuck you think you are. On whoever the fuck you show up as. I don't give a shit who you think you are, I just look at what you do to me, and how you respect me. *(looks at Charles)* Got that, Asshole?
Charles	Roger . . .
Robert	No, it's not Roger, you fuck-face, it's Robert . . .

Robert exits, slamming the front door loudly.

Charles	I meant . . .
Tom	Phew.
Will	My God.
Tom	He actually took our wallets!
Will	Yes, he really did.
Tom	It wasn't . . .
Virginia	It wasn't an act, was it?

Wanda	No, that was real cash. Real credit cards.
Virginia	Has that happened before?
Tom	No, never.
Will	No, it's the first time. I . . . I don't understand. Of course, it could be improv.
Tom	Didn't feel like it.
Wanda	No, it didn't. What a horrible first night.
Tom	You can say that again. I'll never think of that term in the same way again . . . 'First night' . . . Like a kind of blind moment.
Charles	We learned how to be, we thought we knew what would happen, but you can't predict things, can you?
Virginia	Are we almost done now?
Understudy	Yes, is it almost over?
Will	Let me look to see if the coast is clear. *(leaves through the passageway stage right and comes straight back)* He's gone. Well and truly. Not anywhere in sight.
Tom	Not even back there?
Will	No, not even back there.
Tom	Did you see him before?
Will	I believe so. I remember him.
Tom	But like this?
Clarissa	Memory is a hard thing to remember.
Tom	Yes, we may have been so caught up in our own thing that we weren't paying much attention to . . .
Charles	To our fellow . . . to . . . others. It's an important idea. We must pay more attention in the future. We'll have a better chance if we do that.

Virginia	It was real, then, wasn't it?
Tom	I think it may have been. But we can't recall what we should have known. Then again, who knows what's real any more? I mean, one moment we're at peace, everything is okay, then all of a sudden reality changes on us and we're the object of some unknown terrorist group. I think it's best to try to forget what has happened here. We have to recover. I think what happened never happened. We may have imagined this all. It could just as well be theatre.
Will	Yes, we should just all forget about it.
Wanda	Yes, forget about it. But do we vote?
Tom	Where?
Wanda	In elections. Do we vote, or should we forget about that too?
Charles	Um. I got you. No, we should not vote, at least for years. No memory. We must empty our minds. That is freedom. We are best knowing nothing. What's going on is too powerful for us and it's unfair. We have to help ourselves and each other.
Virginia	*(anxiously)* Uh . . . should we be talking about this now, then? I know we're confused, but was this in . . .
Wanda	The uh . . .
Will	Uh . . . I know what you mean.

All the cast members now look out at the audience, stealthily, and each in his or her own way.

Virginia	You know, personally, I think I've had enough.
Tom	Yes, personally, me too.
Charles	I think we've all been through a lot and I'm sure we can go, even if it's not written in stone.
Tom	Yes, even if it's not written down.

Virginia   After all, if it's just been in our minds, if it was like in a
            play or something like that, then we can say it's over, that
            we've had enough, that's fine, right?

*The entire cast rushes through the passageway stage right and exits. The
lights remain on and the curtain does not fall for at least 30 seconds. Then
the lights go out.*

Apply Within

A play in one act

Cast

Manuel Dirsk

Samantha Redden

Sam Crepe

Umwella Spencer

Boris Bezersky

Fred Rachman

Monica Wood

Wilson Fong

Amanda Filch

Gretchen Filch

Cliff Nexton

An interview room which contains only a desk, two chairs and a calendar on the wall. There is a door stage right. Manuel Dirsk – middle-aged, dressed in a worn suit – is sitting at the desk. He appears fatigued and his movements are rather slow.

There is a knock at the door.

Dirsk   Yes.

Another soft knock.

Dirsk   *(irritated)* I've said 'yes', but to get into this room you actually have to open the door!

Samantha Redden enters nervously. She is an attractive woman in her thirties, very smartly dressed in a suit.

Redden   Oh, hi!

Dirsk   Hi?

Redden   *(stopped in her tracks)* Oh . . . ? *(pauses, reassembles her clothing, as if this is the problem)* Oh . . . *(more composed)* Hello.

Dirsk   Um. *(studying her)* Sit down.

Redden   *(moves to the only chair available)* Here?

Dirsk   Where else? *(to himself)* Jesus Christ!

Redden   Yes, of course.

There is a long pause. She sits on the edge of her seat, looking at Dirsk as if he has an answer to her paralysis.

Dirsk   So . . . why are you here?

Redden   I'm an applicant.

Dirsk   Yes, of course, an applicant. Why?

Redden   Why have I applied?

Dirsk   *(wearily)* I ask the questions. Give me your best answer.

Redden   Uh . . . well . . . *(pauses and crosses her legs, staring at Dirsk as though at a complete loss)*

Dirsk   You don't seem to know.

Redden   Know?

Dirsk   You don't seem to know.

Redden   *(as if under a spell)* No . . . I don't. I don't know anything.

Dirsk   So, therefore you are an applicant.

Redden   Yes.

Dirsk   Are you qualified?

Redden   I . . .

Dirsk   You have no qualifications?

Redden   I may.

Dirsk   But you don't know, do you?

Redden   No, I don't. Honestly.

Dirsk   That's admirable. *(shuffles papers, looks bored)* Well, that's it then.

Redden   It?

Dirsk   Yes, thank you for being honest, but we have no need for your services.

Redden   You don't?

Dirsk   I think not.

Redden   Um . . . *(pauses, looking around the room as if confused, as though she might be in the wrong place)* What were they?

Dirsk   What?

Redden   *(looks more confident, but still bewildered)* My services.

Dirsk   Your promises?

Redden   Yes!

Dirsk   Yes, what?

Redden   Yes!

Dirsk   Yes, but what? You have enthusiasm, but for what?

Redden   For this, I think.

Dirsk   What part of this?

Redden   For the . . . for the . . . for the . . .

Dirsk   You don't know what to say, do you?

Redden   I could find something to say.

Dirsk   How?

Redden   With help.

Dirsk   With what kind of help?

Redden   Uh . . . I . . . uh . . .

Dirsk   What are you suggesting?

Redden   Suggesting?

Dirsk   Yes, are you suggesting something?

Redden   Me? Suggesting something?

Dirsk	Yes, are you suggesting that in order to get to the next stage, I have to help you . . . help you in a way that you imply but refuse to state clearly?
Redden	I'm not being clear?
Dirsk	What do you think?
Redden	I agree. I am confused.
Dirsk	Well then.

Triumphantly, Dirsk gets up and walks about. But he is bored now and his speech seems dissociated from the events.

	So . . . you are confused.
Redden	*(now really confused and flustered)* Yes.
Dirsk	And you call yourself an applicant?
Redden	Am I wrong?
Dirsk	An applicant FOR WHAT?
Redden	For what?
Dirsk	Yes, for what? Do you think you're really applying for this position?
Redden	The position I applied for?
Dirsk	Yes. You think this is really for you, or for them? *(points to the door)*
Redden	I . . . I . . . I . . .
Dirsk	Don't know, do you?
Redden	*(crumples up)* No.
Dirsk	OKAY. The door is just there. We'll be in touch. Good luck.

Redden gets up as if lifting a weight, and walks slowly backwards towards the door, keeping her eye on Dirsk. Just before she gets to the door, she faces round, grabs the handle, and then turns back again to Dirsk, as if she is about to say something. He replies by putting his finger to his lips, whereupon Redden exits quickly. Dirsk returns to his desk, shuffles some papers and briefly scans the next applicant's documentation.

Next!

The door flings open and Sam Crepe enters the room. He is in his twenties, casually dressed but very polished. He appears to be too confident, revealing a clear layer of vulnerability.

Crepe   Hi, good to meet you!

He walks up to Dirsk and extends his hand. Dirsk obliges and then slumps in his chair.

Dirsk   So, you're an applicant.

Crepe   You betcha!

Crepe is still standing and Dirsk motions for him to sit down.

Dirsk   And you will tell me what you have to offer?

Crepe   Absolutely.

Dirsk   Good.

Crepe leans forward and is about to launch into his speech when Dirsk puts up his hand.

Just a minute.

Crepe   Sure thing.

Dirsk   Absolutely.

Crepe   What?

Dirsk   You said 'absolutely'.

Crepe   I did?

Dirsk   Yes. So when you think of 'absolutely', what comes into your mind? What do you mean by this?

Crepe	By 'absolutely'?
Dirsk	Yes, absolutely!
Crepe	Ah! *(laughs, thinking they are now on the same wavelength)* Okay. Well, I mean that I'm completely committed and I have no doubt.
Dirsk	No doubt.
Crepe	Yes, no doubt.
Dirsk	About what?
Crepe	About what?
Dirsk	Yes, about what?
Crepe	No doubt about what?
Dirsk	Yes, about what do you have no doubt?
Crepe	I'm not . . . What do you . . . Sorry to be . . . What do you mean?
Dirsk	What do I mean? I thought you were supposed to be the one without doubt?
Crepe	No. I have no doubts.
Dirsk	Well then, go on.
Crepe	I am sure of things.
Dirsk	What things?
Crepe	Of things.
Dirsk	What sort of things?
Crepe	I am sure . . . What sort of things?
Dirsk	You are asking ME?
Crepe	Well . . .

Dirsk	I thought you said when you came into the room that you were an absolutist. You were absolute in your stand as a candidate, but now you seem full of doubt.
Crepe	No . . . *(looks very crushed)*
Dirsk	No?
Crepe	Well . . . yes.
Dirsk	No, yes, no, yes? What is it to be?
Crepe	Uh . . .
Dirsk	*(points to the door)* Well, good luck.

Crepe gets up very quickly and rushes out of the room, clearly relieved to be escaping.

NEXT!

Umwella Spencer, in her mid-thirties, is dressed like a hooker. She is chewing gum, and she moves through the room as if she is casing a joint. She walks past Dirsk, ignoring him, and looks at the calendar on the wall behind his desk. She then turns round and peeks at Dirsk, who has also turned round to see what she is doing. She giggles and Dirsk looks dumbfounded. She then walks round the room looking at nothing, as if it is interesting, and in a few moments sits down in front of Dirsk, who is nonplussed.

Dirsk	Well! *(stares at her intently; Spencer does not reply)* I said 'well'.
Spencer	Yes, I know.
Dirsk	Well?
Spencer	Well, what?
Dirsk	You're the next applicant.
Spencer	What for?
Dirsk	What for?

Spencer   Yes, I mean . . . what for?

Dirsk   You expect me to answer a question like that?

Spencer   You can't?

Dirsk   Can't?

Spencer   You're not UP to it? *(giggles and blows him a kiss)*

Dirsk   I certainly am!

Spencer   Then what am I here for?

Dirsk   You're applying for the position.

Spencer   Or I wouldn't be here.

Dirsk   Yes, or you wouldn't be here.

Spencer   *(sexily)* . . . would I?

Dirsk   No . . . *(confused by her tone and behaviour)* You . . .
wouldn't.

Spencer   So THAT is why I'm here.

Dirsk   *(still confused)* Because?

Spencer   I am applying.

Dirsk   Yes, of course.

Spencer   It's obvious.

She puts both her hands on the desk and leans forward. Dirsk moves back ever so slightly.

Dirsk   Yes, indeed.

Spencer   Indeed.

There is a long pause.

Dirsk   So . . . what have you to say for yourself?

Spencer   Well . . . *(coyly)* It has been said that I am attractive.

Dirsk   *(confused)* That you are attractive?

Spencer   Yes, it has.

Dirsk   References?

Spencer   You want references?

Dirsk   I need substantiation.

Spencer   Oh, I get it. Substantiation. OKAY.

She gets out of her chair with a sort of leap, walks slowly about the room in a kind of spell, throws her shawl on the floor and begins to strip.

Dirsk   *(half-heartedly, because he is entranced by her)* I don't mean that kind of substantiation.

Spencer   What, darling?

Without looking at Dirsk, who is still in a kind of trance, she removes her blouse and skirt.

Dirsk   I don't mean this!

Spencer   *(points to her body)* What IS this?

Dirsk   You know what I mean.

Spencer   You don't know substantiation when you see it? *(laughs heartily)*

Dirsk   That is not what I meant!

She stops stripping and stands, hands on her hips, staring at Dirsk. She is now quite angry.

Spencer   How would you know what you meant until you had fully experienced it?

Dirsk   I'm sure of myself.

Spencer   *(with withering sarcasm)* Mind if I try to apply myself? *(picks up her clothing)*

Dirsk   To what end, may I ask?

Spencer   To THE end, you arrogant prick!

Dirsk   I . . .

Spencer   Oh, don't 'I' me!

Dirsk walks to the door and opens it. Spencer, in the doorway, now talks both to Dirsk and to those in the waiting area, off-stage.

> You're not one to eye anyone, you creep. You just destroy dreams. You're the anti-dream! And you kill those who dream. You are damned.

Spencer leaves, slamming the door. Dirsk stares after her for a moment and then slowly returns to his desk and sits back down.

Dirsk   *(to himself)* What does she mean, I'm the anti-dream? I just didn't know what she meant by substantiation. I didn't know why she was stripping. What for?

He looks around, as if someone in the room could answer the question. He waits about twenty seconds, looks at the next file and talks to himself in a lowered voice.

> Boris Bezersky. Bezersky. So, who are you, then? Whoever are you? I am, I guess, on the verge of finding out. *(loudly)* Next!

Bezersky is a man in his fifties. He enters the room so silently and quickly that he manages to sit in the chair while Dirsk is still reading the file, so Dirsk has not actually seen him.

> Next!

Bezersky clears his throat softly. Dirsk is startled and jumps back slightly in his chair.

> I didn't hear you come in. *(waits, expecting a response but none is forthcoming)* So you are Boris . . . ah . . . Bezersky. *(pronounces it 'Boosirsky')*

Bezersky	No, I am Boris BEZERSKY.
Dirsk	Yes.
Bezersky	No.
Dirsk	No, what?
Bezersky	I am not Boris Boosirsky.
Dirsk	I didn't say you were.
Bezersky	I'm afraid you did.
Dirsk	Well, it's a matter of pronunciation. Surely you have people calling you by different pronunciations?
Bezersky	And I correct them.
Dirsk	All right, fine. I stand corrected. But we're not here for my elocution lesson, but for your application. So . . . I'm waiting. Tell me why you're here.
Bezersky	Of course, that is the question, isn't it.
Dirsk	That much IS obvious, yes.
Bezersky	I understand.
Dirsk	Excellent. *(pauses, taps his pencil on the desk and glares at Bezersky)* Well?
Bezersky	I play the piano.
Dirsk	What?
Bezersky	I play the piano.
Dirsk	Yes, I heard you. But what has that got to do with this?
Bezersky	It has great potential.
Dirsk	For what?
Bezersky	For the position.

Dirsk   It's completely irrelevant to the position.

Bezersky I don't see how this could be true.

Bezersky reaches into his briefcase, takes out a portable tape player and sets it up to play.

Dirsk   What are you doing?

Bezersky Well, I knew you would not have a piano here.

Dirsk   Why ever should we?

Bezersky I hope to show you why.

Dirsk   This is not relevant.

Bezersky Rachmaninoff is irrelevant? His Preludes are certainly not irrelevant. They are a vital part of our lives.

Dirsk   If I say they are irrelevant to this application then my word is the final word on the matter.

Ignoring Dirsk, Bezersky proceeds to play the Fourth Prelude in its entirety. (It is amplified by stage speakers.) The performance is lilting and beautiful and Dirsk moves from clear fidgety irritation, fussing through his papers, to finally being spellbound and enraptured by the music. He crosses his arms and places them on the desk and rests his head on them, face down. When the music stops he remains silent for half a minute. He sits up slowly, takes a handkerchief from his pocket, and wipes his eyes. He has clearly been moved to tears.

     (slowly and haltingly) That was beautiful.

Bezersky *(also moved, speaking slowly)* Yes, it was.

Dirsk   What was it again?

Bezersky Rachmaninoff, Prelude No. 4.

Dirsk   And it was you playing?

Bezersky Yes.

Dirsk	You're very talented.
Bezersky	Yes, I know.
Dirsk	Extraordinary. *(still spellbound, but then he snaps out of it and sits up very straight)* Well, Mr Bezersky, clearly you play the piano superbly. And if this position called for a piano player, then you would be given very serious consideration indeed. But we have no need for it, or for you. I'm sorry.
Bezersky	No need?
Dirsk	No, no need.
Bezersky	But I've just seen a need fulfilled.
Dirsk	What?
Bezersky	I've just seen a need fulfilled.
Dirsk	What sort of need and where?
Bezersky	The need of a man to hear great music.
Dirsk	I have no such need.
Bezersky	Clearly you do.
Dirsk	What do you mean, CLEARLY I do?
Bezersky	Hearing the Prelude transformed you from a tired, irritated and directionless man into an enraptured and meditative being. It changed you before my eyes.
Dirsk	Well, so would the arrival of an articulated lorry smashing through the wall there.
Bezersky	Well, maybe you need someone to arrange such an event. Obviously it cannot be good for you to be cooped up in this room all day, every day, interviewing applicants.
Dirsk	That's my concern, not yours.
Bezersky	I am not so sure.

Dirsk	Well, I am.
Bezersky	I think your certainty is part of the problem. Your certainty constitutes an obstacle for all the people who walk into this room. All applicants are affected by your certainty. It puts people off.
Dirsk	What are you, a social worker?
Bezersky	I expect you will never know the answer to that question. It would seem I'm on the verge of being dismissed.
Dirsk	Ah, in that respect you are quite right. Astute of you.
Bezersky	*(getting up and walking to the door)* Well. This will have been memorable, of that I am sure. *(he is out of the door as Dirsk tries to respond)*
Dirsk	Memorable . . . ? What do . . . What the hell did he mean by that? Memorable, WHAT is memorable? None of this shit is memorable. That's the problem. *(pauses)* Well, maybe he meant the Rachmaninoff. *(laughs)* Imagine that! Rachmaninoff! Maybe that is what we need. *(laughs and then yells with some gusto)* Next!

Fred Rachman enters. He is in his late thirties, dressed in a slick suit, and he carries a large briefcase. He is rather stiff and arrogant.

	Please sit down.
Rachman	Thank you.
Dirsk	*(looking at the sheet in front of him)* You are Rachman, is that right?
Rachman	Yes.
Dirsk	Well, that is a relief.
Rachman	A relief?
Dirsk	It's a relief that you are who you claim to be.
Rachman	Someone else claimed to be me?

Dirsk	Did I say that?
Rachman	I think it is inferable.
Dirsk	How is that possible?
Rachman	Well, if you are surprised that I am who I say I am, then it seems possible that someone else appeared here who said they were me, when it fact they weren't me at all.
Dirsk	Well, that's odd thinking, very odd. It would seem to me far more likely that I was referring to someone else who did not appear to be who they claimed to be. I've no idea why you leapt to the conclusion that I might be referring to you.
Rachman	Because I'm in the room with you.
Dirsk	What has that got to do with it?
Rachman	I assumed that you made this comment because someone had impersonated me and you were glad that here I am in the flesh, true Rachman that I am.
Dirsk	True Rachman that you are?
Rachman	I'm sorry?
Dirsk	What does this mean, true Rachman that you are? True Rachman? What are you talking about?
Rachman	I am the true Rachman, not someone else.
Dirsk	Well, how could you ever have been someone else?
Rachman	Well, Rachman is a changed name.
Dirsk	What?
Rachman	It's short for Rachmaninoff.
Dirsk	*(jumping out of his chair)* Rachmaninoff!
Rachman	You seem shocked.

Dirsk	I am totally shocked. *(sits back down in his chair)*
Rachman	Why? Names are shortened all the time.
Dirsk	Not like this, they're not.
Rachman	Like what?
Dirsk	I've just been listening to Rachmaninoff.
Rachman	What?
Dirsk	Here, just two minutes before you entered the room.
Rachman	That's impossible.
Dirsk	What's impossible?
Rachman	Rachmaninoff is dead.
Dirsk	Of course he's dead, you idiot.
Rachman	Yet you claim he was just in the room with you.
Dirsk	His music, his music was just in the room with me.
Rachman	*(looking around the room)* Well, I see no piano, or CD player, and you don't look like the sort of interviewer who takes time for musical interludes.
Dirsk	Well, I did and I recommend it. It works wonders.
Rachman	You don't seem to be in a wonderful state, if you don't mind my saying so.
Dirsk	My state is none of your business.
Rachman	As long as my name is secure, I've no other worries.
Dirsk	What do you mean, secure? How am I responsible for securing your name?
Rachman	If you confused me with someone else, or gave my position to another, assuming it was me you were giving it to, all because you'd forgotten my name, or someone

impersonating Rachmaninoff managed to get the job . . .
That would upset me.

Dirsk   How the hell would you know about it, anyway?

Rachman   Because I would not be here and someone else would be.

Dirsk   So what?

Rachman   Well, they would probably be here because they got the
           job instead of me.

Dirsk   Exactly!

Rachman   By mistaken identity. They got the job instead of ME.

Dirsk   If so, they got the job because they were more qualified
           than you, more suited for the job.

Rachman   Or more wonderful because they stole the name
           Rachmaninoff and you heard bells.

Dirsk   I did not hear bells.

Rachman   Rachmaninoff wrote a work called The Bells. You could
           have heard bells.

Dirsk   I know the piece, but it was not The Bells.

Rachman   What, then?

Dirsk   A Prelude.

Rachman   You heard a Prelude?

Dirsk   *(looks embarrassed)* Yes, No. 4.

Rachman   How did that happen?

Dirsk   The previous applicant played it for me.

Rachman   What? The previous applicant stole my name, then played
           my work for you?

Dirsk   Yes, he played Rachmaninoff, but no, he did not represent
           himself as Rachmaninoff and, anyway, you are not THE

Rachmaninoff – if you are to be believed, you are simply some very distant relative.

Rachman   I'm his great-grandson.

Dirsk   Well, there you go.

Rachman   Where? What do you mean?

Dirsk   You're distant – too distant for this to mean anything.

Rachman   If your name were Rachmaninoff, it would not feel like a distant name to you.

Dirsk   No, you are distant from HIM.

Rachman   Well, not so distant from him that you haven't thought you just saw him a few minutes ago, if I may say so.

Dirsk   I never said that!

Dirsk is about to elaborate but stops himself.

Now look. You're an applicant and you're here to apply for the position. In twenty-five words or less I want to know why you think you're suited for the post.

Suddenly very alert and positive, Rachman speaks in a way that indicates he has clearly rehearsed his lines, and indeed this is why he makes several slips of the tongue.

Rachman   Ah. Yes. I am the man for the post because with my background in the sciences and my previous experience working in PET scan technology I am ill-suited to looking into the hearts of matters. I have been trained to see into people, to isolate patterns of dark mutter, and with my years of doing this every day, I have proven experience in this technology and am wary of its wide ramifications. *(sits back, beaming)*

Dirsk   Do you realise you said you were 'ill-suited' to look into the hearts of matters?

Rachman   I said I was 'suited' to look into the hearts of matters.

Dirsk	Actually, no, you made a rather unfortunate slip. You also said you looked into the hearts of the 'mutter'.
Rachman	Matter.
Dirsk	Actually, you said 'mutter'.
Rachman	*(reaches into his pocket, pulls out an index card and hands it to Dirsk)* Well, look – read it yourself. You will see what I said.
Dirsk	*(takes the card, glances at it, and quickly drops it on the table)* Look, you are not for us. You had to prepare a speech that anyone should have been able to say without this kind of coaching. Further, you couldn't even recall it properly and made several crucial errors. I think you spoke the truth when you said you were ill-suited for this position. Goodbye.
Rachman	This is deeply unfair.
Dirsk	Unfair?
Rachman	Profoundly so.
Dirsk	How so?
Rachman	You've twisted my words, you've allowed another applicant to steal my name, and now without any further ado, you just . . . what . . . dismiss me? That's it?
Dirsk	Yes.
Rachman	But you can't. Not like this!
Dirsk	And why not?
Rachman	Because it's not right.
Dirsk	It is my JOB, you idiot. I can dismiss anyone I want. I can order them to turn around when they come in the door and yell 'OUT' and they have to leave. You are the applicants and not me. I can do anything I want. So get the fuck out of here, I'm tired of your whining.

Rachman   *(gets up abruptly, kicks the chair, walks in broad steps to the door and turns around)* Well, you call me the idiot, but it's you who have lost a Rachmaninoff! *(slams the door as he exits)*

Dirsk   Lost a Rachmaninoff? Hah! What a complete fool. *(pauses)* Well, he's right in one sense. I loved that Prelude. Old what's-his-name was correct – it is memorable. I can still hear it. It's inside me. And God, do I need this today. Now, who is . . . next? *(shuffles through his papers)* Ah . . . well, a woman. I've had enough of tough bastards for today. *(loudly)* NEXT.

A middle-aged woman enters, dressed in a loose-fitting flowery outfit and carrying a big knitted bag. She walks up confidently and sits in the chair.

Wood   Hello, I am Monica Wood.

Dirsk   Yes, I know.

Wood   That's good.

Dirsk   It's my job.

Wood   Of course it is, and a very good job it must be.

Dirsk   I don't know about that, but it is what I do.

Wood   Hard day?

Dirsk   Well, I've had easier.

Wood   Oh . . . poor you.

Dirsk   *(taken aback somewhat)* No, it's nothing..

Wood   Well, look at your desk.

Dirsk   My desk?

Wood   It's all a mess, isn't it?

She gets up and starts to tidy his papers. Dirsk is quite startled. In a few moments Wood has arranged his papers into a pile and put his pen and pencils in a black holder. She takes what looks like a newspaper, gazes at it and dumps it in the dustbin next to the desk.

Dirsk   Really . . . And that was my newspaper.

Wood   Yesterday's! Poor you. Anyway, think nothing of it. Just relax, it will be over with in a minute. How can a man expect to interview people when his desk is all a mess?

She takes a stapler, a staple remover, loose files and other sundries and puts them in a black tray on top of the desk.

            There! Done! *(sits back down)*

Dirsk   Well . . . uh . . . now . . .

Wood   The job.

Dirsk   Yes. The job.

Wood   What am I supposed to do?

Dirsk   Tell me why you've applied.

Wood   Because I'm helpful.

Dirsk   In what ways?

Wood   Well . . . Oh – now look! *(points to one side of his desktop)*

Dirsk   What?

Wood   That's awful.

Dirsk   What's awful?

Wood   No one should have to work on a desk that's stained like that.

She brings out an aerosol can and a rag from her bag and immediately sprays the area, before vigorously rubbing the rag over the desk. Dirsk pushes his chair back and stares in utter amazement.

            There we go, end of problem.

Dirsk	Did you come prepared?
Wood	Prepared?
Dirsk	Did you come intentionally with the desk cleaner and the cloth?
Wood	Intentionally?
Dirsk	Yes, did you intend to do this to me?
Wood	No . . . not to my knowledge.
Dirsk	Well, who would know, then?
Wood	Well, I didn't know you had a desk. But you know that you do. So, is it possible that it was to your knowledge?
Dirsk	What, that you would clean my desk?
Wood	It was dirty and needed cleaning.
Dirsk	You're suggesting that I left my desk unclean so that someone, some applicant, would take it upon himself or herself to clean my desk for me?
Wood	Well, it is a job application, isn't it?
Dirsk	You think part of the job is to clean my desk?
Wood	Isn't it?
Dirsk	Well, why?
Wood	I don't know. Is it a test?
Dirsk	A test?
Wood	Is it a test, the dirty desk?
Dirsk	A test of what?
Wood	Of whether I could do the job.
Dirsk	But WHAT job?
Wood	You don't know what job you're offering?

Dirsk   What?

Wood   You just said . . . I'm so sorry, but you just said 'What
            job?' and it looked like you didn't know what job you were
            offering your applicants. I am sorry if I misunderstood
            you.

*Dirsk is halted by her apology and adjusts his tie. He runs his hands
through his hair, gently touches the part of his desk that has been cleaned,
brings his hands together in a kind of unconscious praying position, and
looks calmly into Wood's eyes.*

Dirsk   Mrs . . .

Wood   Miss.

Dirsk   Miss Wood. *(very calmly and slowly)* Please take your time
            and tell me in twenty-five words or less why you think
            you're qualified to fill the position for which I am
            interviewing you. Take your time and do not rush things.

Wood   I like looking after people. I have been a carer for some
            years – I looked after the dying, which I found fulfilling. I
            also love purchasing things and I would love to be part of
            the purchasing side of the job. I also love cleaning and
            would WANT to help you if you were part of the job.
            (hesitates and looks up to the ceiling, close to tears) I guess . . .
            I guess . . . I just care. I'm sorry.

*She takes out a handkerchief, pats her eyes and blows her nose. Dirsk is
clearly at a loss. He stares at Wood, who now stares back. Some moments
pass.*

Dirsk   OKAY. Thank you for your answer. It's good to know that
            you are a carer and that you have looked after the dying.
            That is admirable, but . . . and please, if you can answer
            briefly and if it upsets you, well then don't bother to
            answer, but what does looking after the dying have to do
            with the job?

Wood   You don't think someone is dying on the job?

Dirsk	What?
Wood	No one is dying?
Dirsk	Where?
Wood	Here.
Dirsk	Where is 'here'? *(points around the room)* Here?
Wood	In the workplace. There is no one dying?
Dirsk	Well, how would I know?
Wood	It would be my job to know and to look after them.
Dirsk	What, on the job?
Wood	I'm good at that.
Dirsk	At what? Looking after the dying at work?
Wood	That's a good idea, isn't it! You are creative to have thought that up. Surely that is needed and what a job this is, then.
Dirsk	That was not my idea, it was yours!
Wood	Looking after the dying at work?
Dirsk	It was your idea, not mine.
Wood	That's so sweet of you to say that. I think this must be a lesson in creative management. I've read that the best bosses make it look like all the creative ideas have come from the staff when in fact they've come from the bosses. And you, clever man, have done that with me.
Dirsk	Miss . . .
Wood	Wood.
Dirsk	Miss Wood. We do not have a job here for someone to look after the dying in the workplace. And the job has not been defined as part of purchasing. We also have cleaners and there is no need for you to volunteer to do the cleaning.

Wood	Well – what is the job, then?
Dirsk	That is not for me to tell you. It is expected of the applicants that through their own independent research they will be familiar with the job on offer, they will have prepared their credentials and presented us with a reason why they should be offered the particular position.
Wood	*(stunned)* You mean, I'm not going to get the job?
Dirsk	Well, how can you? You don't even know what it is!
Wood	*(puts her face in her handkerchief and starts to cry)* Oh, whatever am I going to do?
Dirsk	*(walks over to her, puts his arm around her and gently leads her to the door as he speaks)* You're a very good person, Miss Wood. I'm sure you will find the right job for you one of these days. I'm sure those who are dying can do with more of your caretaking, and as for purchasing, maybe you should take yourself out and buy something to give you a treat. Bye bye.

She slips through the door. Dirsk walks slowly back to his desk, puts his hands on top of his head, twirls around a few times, and does a bit of exercising. He sits down in his chair, opens up the next application and then drops it.

Next!

A young man in his twenties, casually dressed in jeans and a Hawaiian shirt, enters the room. He waits briefly at the door and waves his hand in a kind of Native American greeting, but avoids eye contact. He looks at the floor as he walks very slowly and tentatively to the chair, and sits down gingerly. He looks at the desk rather than at Dirsk.

So you are . . . ?

Fong	My name is Wilson Fong.
Dirsk	Good. Glad you have a name.

Fong   *(laughs uncomfortably)* Yeah, me too.

Dirsk   Yes, we need them, don't we?

Fong   Yeah . . . tell me about it. And some are easier to come by.

Dirsk   Sorry?

Fong   I mean, some names are easier to come by. *(looks up at Dirsk very briefly and then looks at the desk again)*

Dirsk   I don't quite get the drift. You . . . What . . . Did you change your name . . . or purchase it, or something like that?

Fong   Well . . . 'Wilson Fong' is a kind of contradiction.

Dirsk   Because . . . ?

Fong   Well, as you see, I'm not Asian, and Fong is a Chinese name.

Dirsk   Yes, that had occurred to me.

Fong   *(laughing nervously)* I think it kind of occurs to everyone. *(glances up at Dirsk, then again stares at the desktop)*

Dirsk   So you are experienced in such matters.

Fong   Yes, that is well said. Yes. When I have to introduce myself it is always a bit unclear how I will be received, given my name and all.

Dirsk   Sure. Well, here at least, it doesn't matter.

Fong   It doesn't?

Fong now looks up and occasionally glances at Dirsk, but he remains uncomfortable and is unable to maintain sustained eye contact.

Dirsk   Not in the least.

Fong   Not at all?

Dirsk   Absolutely not.

Fong	But . . . *(confused, he very suddenly looks sharply down at his feet, as if he has lost something)*
Dirsk	Have you lost something?
Fong	No.
Dirsk	But something has happened, is that right?
Fong	Well . . . it's kind of embarrassing. *(he is back to looking at the desktop)*
Dirsk	Oh.
Fong	Yeah.
Dirsk	Do you need anything?
Fong	I beg your pardon?
Dirsk	Would it be better if I left the room? Or . . . I've a better idea . . . The men's room is just down the hall on your left, about fifty feet.
Fong	What would I find there?
Dirsk	A loo.
Fong	Yeah, but . . . why are you suggesting I go there? *(glances up anxiously for a moment, then looks back at the desktop)*
Dirsk	Uh, because I thought you had, you know, had an accident.
Fong	An accident? *(glances up briefly again, then looks back at the desktop)*
Dirsk	Yes, in a manner of speaking.
Fong	What kind of accident?
Dirsk	The kind that would necessitate your going to the loo.
Fong	But if I'd had an accident, wouldn't I go to hospital or something like that?

Dirsk	What?
Fong	If I'd had the accident you thought I had, wouldn't I go to hospital?
Dirsk	What, for shitting yourself?
Fong	I beg your pardon?
Dirsk	You have shit yourself, am I right?
Fong	Oh . . . do I . . . smell? *(looks up briefly at Dirsk before once again focusing on the desk)*
Dirsk	No.
Fong	But I give you the impression of . . . Do you think I'm full of shit?
Dirsk	I don't know. Not yet, at least.
Fong	Because that's possible, you know.
Dirsk	What is?
Fong	It's possible that I'm full of shit.
Dirsk	Hardly a strong card to play in a moment like this, is it?
Fong	Well, I reckoned you'd come to this conclusion. Why should I hide it? I'm applying for this job and frankly I think I'm probably not the guy for the job.
Dirsk	How do you know?
Fong	Because I do think I'm full of it. I could try to convince you I am the right person for this position, but frankly I haven't a clue what this job is about. All I saw was 'Job available, apply within' and like a dog on a leash I just walked in, filled in the application form, and here I am.
Dirsk	Well, indeed. Here you are.
Fong	And you already know I'm full of crap, right?

Dirsk	Well, I don't know that. I thought you had actually shit yourself.
Fong	But I've just told you I'm full of shit, so . . .
Dirsk	So . . . what? So what?
Fong	Well, what kind of job is it that you want to hire someone who's full of it? *(looks up at Dirsk then back at the desktop)*
Dirsk	Ah! That's brilliant! That's the best question I have ever had from anyone.
Fong	Well, I'm glad that a guy like me can make a small contribution on this planet before . . .
Dirsk	Before what?
Fong	Before he goes to the waste disposal unit.
Dirsk	What?
Fong	You know.
Dirsk	I know what?
Fong	Before I'm done.
Dirsk	Done?
Fong	Before there's no reason for me to be here any more.
Dirsk	Suicide? Are you talking of killing yourself?
Fong	How confidential is our meeting?
Dirsk	Completely. Completely.
Fong	Well, actually, when I saw 'apply within', I was on my way to the bridge because I thought I would jump. There is no point to my life. I AM full of shit. There IS no hope. My mind is a colonoscopy bag. People think I think. In fact, my mind is a secret shithouse. When I get into what seem like real conversations with people, I can see the thought

come over their face, 'this guy is full of shit' and that's TRUE, so who wants to live with this fact?

Dirsk   It doesn't seem like a fact. It seems like you are remarkably – in fact, disturbingly – honest about yourself. You do not seem like someone who's full of shit. But I have noticed that you won't look at me, but prefer to talk to my desk.

Fong   That's what being full of bullshit looks like.

Dirsk   What?

Fong   If you're FULL of it then however much you can appear to be interesting, you can appear to know a lot, you can appear to know the right people, you can appear to know the right places to eat, the right books to read, you are . . . you see . . . you're still just full of bull. And you can't look another human in the face, because you know this about yourself.

Dirsk   So you know nothing? Your application form is full of lies?

Fong   No, not lies. I do know a lot. At university I did intellectual history, I did an MA in philosophy and another MA in computer design. I have worked for a lot of people. Tons of people love me. You wouldn't think so at first sight, would you?

Dirsk   No, you struck me as somehow . . .

Fong   Nerdish.

Dirsk   Yes, rather.

Fong   You're an honest man.

Fong now looks up from the desk and maintains an on/off eye contact with Dirsk.

Dirsk   I try to be.

Fong   You're NOT full of shit, are you?

Dirsk   I wouldn't say so, no. I don't actually think this is a useful
          way to think.

Fong   But in your job, with all these applicants, you don't think
          to yourself that so-and-so is full of shit?

Dirsk   Oh yes, all the time.

Fong   Well then, so you do think like that.

Dirsk   I suppose you're right. I'd not realised it until now. *(there is
          a long pause as he sizes up Fong)* So . . . tell me . . . why are
          you saying all of this? If you hope for this job, why are you
          in effect asking to be rejected?

Fong   Because I'm full of crap and you smelled it. An honest
          man like you deserves an honest reply.

Dirsk   Oh, come on, now. This is becoming tiresome and it's no
          explanation.

Fong   But it's true. To be more precise, there is nothing I say
          which I actually believe in. If you do not believe in any
          of your thoughts, if you do not believe in any of your
          statements, if you do not believe in any of your relations,
          then everything is shit. But one must accept the
          conclusion that one is full of crap oneself – not others.

Dirsk   So . . . uh . . .

Fong   What do we do?

Dirsk   Yes, what . . .

Fong   The obvious.

Dirsk   Which is?

Fong   I have to tell you your job?

Dirsk   I say to you to go . . .

Fong   . . . because you cannot be bothered.

Dirsk	*(shakes his head, pushes his chair back, scrutinises Fong)* Okay. You know, I agree with you. I DO think you're full of shit.
Fong	Thanks for believing in me.
Dirsk	I don't believe in you.
Fong	Thanks for that.
Dirsk	I want you to get out of this room and I don't want to see you again!
Fong	You can't take any more of this shit.
Dirsk	No, I can't.
Fong	I understand. Please . . .
Dirsk	Please what?
Fong	I need silence now.

Fong holds up his hand as he sees Dirsk is about to speak. Then he rises from the chair and walks slowly to the door, puts his finger to his lips in a continued non-verbal 'ssshh' sound, and closes the door very quietly on his way out. Dirsk gets up and walks round the room.

Dirsk	Well. Well . . . fuck that. What the fuck? What was that all about? I mean, the guy WAS full of shit, right? *(pauses)* Well, he couldn't have been, could he? He was a fucking saint in some respects. Who else has been here and talked like that? Everyone I've seen is full of bullshit and yet he's the first one to say so. He's a fucking Jesus Christ, and now he's going to jump into the river. *(pacing up and down the room)* What the hell was I supposed to do? It's not my fault, is it? It can't be. The first honest bastard who comes in here and what . . . he says he's full of crap. So he couldn't possibly have been offered the job. But he should have been, shouldn't he? He should have been given the job straight off, but it isn't yours to do that, is it? You only interview the applicants, you have NO AUTHORITY to

do anything other than that. You don't even know what the fucking job is, do you? They claim that's the beauty of the thing. You don't know, the applicants don't know, and somehow out of this PURE ignorance, what they call the 'sacred unknown', an applicant captures the job because he or she is guided to it. So this guy . . . he wasn't guided to it, was he? *(looks out at the audience, worried, as if seeking help)* I mean, he wasn't guided . . . was he? *(walks silently around the room)* No. He didn't say he was guided into the room, he said he saw the 'apply within' sign and just dropped in. He was a drop-in. A drive-by. The fucker shot you. He might just as well have pulled out a Glock and fired the fucker at you. Telling you he's full of shit. What kind of a trick is that? Only someone who is TRULY full of shit would pull that sort of a con. The fucker. If he shows his sick face in here again, I'm going to smash him in.

Dirsk is now walking around the room at a furious pace, but gradually he slows down and then walks to his desk. He sits in his chair for a moment and runs his hands through his hair. He looks very briefly at a file.

Next.

Amanda Filch, who is fifteen, and her mother, Gretchen Filch, in her mid-fifties, walk into the room. They are wearing matching pink dresses and bright red shoes. There is only one free chair, so Gretchen pushes Amanda gently by the shoulders and stands behind her as Amanda sits in the chair.

Amanda and Gretchen   *(in unison)* Hello, Mr Dirsk.

Dirsk   How did you know my name?

Amanda and Gretchen   *(in unison)* We asked.

Dirsk   Whom did you ask?

Amanda and Gretchen   *(in unison)* The doorman.

Dirsk	Weatherspoon?
Amanda	Mother, was it Weatherspoon?
Gretchen	No, darling, it was Havenhurst.
Dirsk	That dumb son of a bitch.
Gretchen	I beg your pardon?
Dirsk	Nothing. Sorry. *(suddenly, as if seeing them for the first time)* What in the . . . heck . . . are the two of you doing in here?
Gretchen	I am her mother.
Dirsk	Who cares? What for?
Gretchen	Who cares? Well, I care. Her father cares. Her two brothers and sister care. As do her friends in school and tons of people. And what for . . .
Dirsk	Oh, forget it . . . ah . . .
Gretchen	Well, how could we? Who could forget that?
Amanda	Mum, it's okay.
Gretchen	No, darling, it is NOT OKAY. The reason we agreed – your father and I – that I had to accompany you was exactly for this, precisely because you could be ABUSED in the process of the job application.
Dirsk	What?
Amanda	Mum, lay off.
Gretchen	I said ABUSED.
Dirsk	What is abusive here? What are you talking about?
Gretchen	When I said I was her mother, you said 'who cares?' and 'what for?' and those lines are not only unforgettable, they are the engines of litigation, that is what they are.

Dirsk	The engines of litigation? Lady, what are you talking about?
Gretchen	Don't you dare call me 'lady'. Darling, did you hear that?
Amanda	Mum . . .
Dirsk	Wait, wait, wait! You say I can't call you 'lady' and yet you call her 'darling'. What if I called her 'darling', what then?
Gretchen	What?
Dirsk	*(to Amanda)* What is your name?
Amanda	*(shyly)* Amanda.
Dirsk	Amanda, what if I were to call you 'darling'? Your mother just did.
Amanda	Well, I . . .
Gretchen	*(opening her handbag and writing in a notebook)* Do you see what I'm doing?
Dirsk	What are you doing?
Gretchen	I'm writing everything down.
Dirsk	Why?
Gretchen	Why? Why?
Dirsk	Yes, WHY?
Gretchen	Because this is clearly an abusive situation. You are violating my daughter's rights. You are treating her inappropriately.

Dirsk checks his response, then gets up, turns around and looks at his calendar, leafing through it briefly. He runs his hand through his hair and then turns around to face Amanda and Gretchen. He smiles broadly but speaks with a false and formal voice, barely able to conceal his contempt.

Dirsk	Miss and Mrs Filch, I do sincerely and wholeheartedly apologise for any unintentional insult I have passed your way.

Gretchen	What?
Amanda	Mum, it's over, he's apologising.
Gretchen	What? What? What's happening?
Dirsk	Mrs Filch, I wish to convey my apology for any misunderstanding that may have occurred. As you see, I am writing this down for you as we talk. *(takes out a pad and writes)* Please read it. *(hands the pad to Gretchen)*
Gretchen	It says 'I apologise on behalf of myself and my institution for any unintended offence caused during the course of this interview', and you add the time: 2.37 p.m. Why do you add the time?
Dirsk	Because you entered the room at 2.30 and you have an apology from me by 2.37.
Amanda	Mum, I think we should leave.
Gretchen	I don't get it. Why the time stuff?
Dirsk	Well, I suggest that you discuss this with your lawyer. What's his name . . . Higgenbottom, Wigglesworth?
Gretchen	Van Axel, if you need to know.
Dirsk	Yes, Van Axel.
Gretchen	You know him?
Dirsk	No.
Gretchen	Then why do you ask?
Dirsk	Well, I love to hear the sound of names, like condensed poems: sort of sonatas in one moment. 'Van Axel' sounds like a part of a lorry that one might need at certain moments. I'm sure he's a good lawyer.
Gretchen	I use him often.
Dirsk	No doubt.

Gretchen	No doubt about what?
Dirsk	Well, Mrs Filch, I do not wish to comment on our situation, so I shall speak only in the abstract.
Amanda	Mum, I think we should get out of here NOW.
Gretchen	Go on, Mr Dirsk.
Dirsk	Once upon a time there was a mother and a child, called Trudy and Troll. Trudy was the daughter and Troll was the mother. Troll did not know what to do with herself, but one day she happened upon the idea that if she could put Trudy in situations with men that she could spy on, then she could threaten these men with lawsuits if they did not treat Trudy with absolute respect.
Gretchen	GOOD FOR HER!
Dirsk	I'm sure. So. Well. That's the end of the story.
Amanda	Mum, I'm leaving.

Amanda gets up in a fury and storms out of the room, leaving Gretchen and Dirsk staring at one another.

Gretchen	Well, you can see what you've done, can't you?
Dirsk	What is that?
Gretchen	That is for me to know and for you . . .
Dirsk	. . . yes, to find out. Goodbye, Mrs Filch.
Gretchen	You will . . .
Dirsk	. . . live to regret this.
Gretchen	You have . . .
Dirsk	. . . taken the words right out of your mouth.

Gretchen is stunned by his cunning anticipation of her response. She twirls around pompously as she throws her coat on, and whirls her scarf around her neck, before slamming into the wall next to the door. She bounces off with remarkable resilience and leaves. Dirsk sits at his desk, head between his hands. Time passes. There is a knock at the door.

    Next.

Cliff Nexton enters the room. Dressed in jeans, a white shirt, a leather coat, and cowboy boots, he is embodied, very relaxed, and curious yet seemingly naïve. Despite this, there is something quietly menacing about him.

    Hello.

Nexton	*(sitting down)* My name is Cliff.
Dirsk	Cliff what?
Nexton	Cliff Nexton. Rhymes with 'Exxon'!
Dirsk	You're full of gas?
Nexton	*(laughs)* Now, you know, I've never heard that one before. That's just great! *(laughs again)*
Dirsk	So, what can we do for you, Mr Nexton?
Nexton	Well, I've come for the job.
Dirsk	Ah yes, that.
Nexton	Yup.
Dirsk	Well, you can't just have it, Mr Nexton. You would have to apply for it.
Nexton	How do I do that?
Dirsk	Well, you're doing it right now.
Nexton	I am?
Dirsk	Yes, sir, you are.
Nexton	Right now?
Dirsk	I reckon so.
Nexton	What am I doing?

Dirsk   You're applying.

Nexton   So, this job . . . uh . . .

Dirsk   Yes?

Nexton   This job that I'm applying for, is . . . uh . . . available,
           is it?

Dirsk   Thus far, yes.

Nexton   That's good! *(looking ebullient, he reaches across the table to
           shake Dirsk's hand, startling him)*

Dirsk   There really is no need for celebration.

Nexton   Well, you see, jobs are so hard to find these days that just
           knowing this job is still open is . . . is . . . well, it's heart-
           warming. I feel GOOD just knowing it's there. I'm
           American and I have a positive outlook on life, so I'm
           happy knowing that things are open here.

Dirsk   Well, I'm glad we can make you feel that way.

Nexton   Darn right. It IS good, isn't it, Mr Dirsk?

Dirsk   Yes, I agree.

Nexton   I bet you want someone who really knows what to do with
           this job, is that right?

Dirsk   I think that's a fair statement.

Nexton   Someone who would know just how to step right in and
           take charge of it.

Dirsk   Well . . . something like that.

Nexton   Ah huh. Well. Maybe not rush in to take charge, but
           perhaps to kind of sit back, study the situation, take
           consultation and then occupy the job. What about that?

Dirsk   Yes, that sounds a bit more like it.

Nexton   And, observing the situation, that person would see just what this job entailed, wouldn't they? They would have to grab the job by the tail.

Nexton gets up out of his chair and wanders about the room, lost in a kind of reverie but every so often looking back at Dirsk, pointing his finger, as if engaged with him.

They would have to see that this was no ordinary job and that no ordinary person could fill it. It would take a person who was sensitive to the job description and who knew its place within the institution. It's the kind of job that has a long history to it and that would need to be studied. It could not just be taken up, like that! No, no, no, no. No. It's no bull to be taken by the horns. It's a job that must first be studied and then gradually occupied. You must occupy it. This job will come with responsibilities. It will have filing cabinets full of its past and pregnant with its future. *(Dirsk reaches into his desk for a pill, which he swallows with a glass of water)* There will be memos from other employees, some of them unanswered. Some of them could have been unanswered for years, so the new job occupant will have to catch up with that past. He will have to apologise to those other employees whose queries or requests have gone unanswered. And I am the man for that kind of duty, sir. I am. I know how to apologise for wrongdoing. Boy do I. The good thing about making big mistakes in life is that one learns how to apologise. And if you have had lots of time to think about those mistakes, you know how to contemplate them, how to run them through the prism of your mind and discover the many small mistakes inside the larger ones. No more bank robbery for me! No more time! *(returns to the chair and sits down)* What do you think, Mr Dirsk, am I the man for this job? *(Dirsk stares speechlessly at him)* Mr Dirsk?

Dirsk slowly and wearily rises to his feet, about to say something, then sits back down and speaks very slowly. He is clearly afraid.

Dirsk	Mr Nexton, I . . . I . . . don't know how to tell you this.
Nexton	Go for it!
Dirsk	Yes. I think your commentary on the job was eloquent and I think we would be privileged to have you fill the position . . .
Nexton	Great!
Dirsk	But, Mr Nexton, we have a policy that forbids us to hire people with a criminal record.
Nexton	*(suddenly becomes menacing)* You what?
Dirsk	We have a policy that, unfortunately, forbids us to hire individuals such as yourself who have served time.
Nexton	Who put that policy into place?
Dirsk	Well, I really don't know.
Nexton	*(raising his voice)* You don't know?
Dirsk	No, I don't. It's just a policy.
Nexton	Well, policies can change, can't they?
Dirsk	Yes, of course, but I am not in a position to do anything about this policy.
Nexton	Why not?
Dirsk	Because this has nothing to do with my function.
Nexton	Well then, partner, I'm telling you. The policy is now changed. That is my function. I'm sure I walked through that door there in order to change this policy. So forget it. Now I'm sure I'm in good hands.
Dirsk	Look, this is absurd. *(Nexton points at him menacingly)* Okay. If in your mind the policy says we now hire ex-cons, so be it.

Nexton	It's not just in MY mind, it's in yours too. *(continues to point at Dirsk, wagging his finger)*
Dirsk	Not really, no.
Nexton	It has to be, you just said it was. *(drops his hand into his lap)*
Dirsk	I complied with you because, frankly, you're a rather scary guy. You could tell me there are Martians in the waiting room and I would not challenge you.
Nexton	So what are you saying?
Dirsk	To my knowledge, next to nothing. Indeed, I hope as close to nothing as is possible.
Nexton	And what does that accomplish?
Dirsk	It reduces my significance.
Nexton	What does that do?
Dirsk	It protects me.
Nexton	*(looking baffled, he sits back in his chair)* Listen, what is your problem? I'm honest enough to tell you I'm an ex-con, you freak out, you finally relent on your idiotic policy, and now you tell me you're afraid of me and that you do not want to have any significance. Where does this put me?
Dirsk	You?
Nexton	Yes, exactly where do you think this puts me?
Dirsk	But you are not 'in my hands', as you said.
Nexton	I certainly am.
Dirsk	No.
Nexton	Yes.

Dirsk	No, you are your own business. I'm not responsible for you.
Nexton	In this room, you are responsible for how you conduct yourself in relation to me, and you've put me in the dark.
Dirsk	How?
Nexton	By disappearing through some fog of words. I don't know what you're talking about.
Dirsk	Look, let me be clear.

Dirsk stands up and gestures to Nexton to do the same. He attempts a kind of false geniality as he quietly walks Nexton to the door.

	You have made an important point. You have insisted that we change the policy on ex-cons and I have HAD to accept that. It was a FORCEFUL point you made and I really agree I had NO ALTERNATIVE but to accept your demand. A man like you, with your strength, is going to go far and who knows, you may even get this job.
Nexton	What do you mean, 'who knows'?
Dirsk	Well, it's not up to me.
Nexton	The appointments are not up to you?
Dirsk	No, the appointments are not up to me. I am responsible for meeting the applicants, but not for anything else.
Nexton	So you don't have any influence over who gets the job, any say-so?
Dirsk	*(tired, bewildered, and now mildly confessional)* No, you know, not only that, but 'they', whoever 'they' are – and I don't know them because I've only met one person here – they've not even told me what the job is.
Nexton	*(yells)* What? *(steps back)* You're telling me that you don't even know what the job is? They haven't told you?
Dirsk	That about sums it up.

Nexton	You poor bastard.
Dirsk	That also about sums it up.
Nexton	Well, I'll be damned. *(opens the door violently, turns round and looks at Dirsk)* You poor DUMB bastard. *(exits)*

Dirsk walks around the room for a few minutes, running his hands through his hair, leaning on the wall, then feeling the desk where it had been cleaned earlier. He does not say anything. Finally he sits down again and stares at the door. He is shocked back into his reality when Samantha Redden opens the door and flounces in, standing some four feet from his desk, smiling broadly.

Redden	Hi, how are you doing?
Dirsk	*(stands up)* Miss, Miss . . .
Redden	Redden.
Dirsk	Miss Redden, you have already been interviewed. You should not be back in this room. I don't know who let you in, but I can't talk to you. Would you just . . . just . . . *(wearily, pointing to the door)* Would you just please leave.
Redden	Oh, you poor man. *(motions to him to sit down, as she sits in the chair opposite)*
Dirsk	No, I'm not a poor man, Miss Redden, but I shall be the poorer for it if you do not do as I have just asked. Whatever is . . .
Redden	I think you're doing a fabulous job.
Dirsk	What? I . . .
Redden	All day, interviewing people for a job, and you have no idea what the job is, do you?
Dirsk	*(angrily)* Well, I suppose that's getting around, isn't it! No, I haven't. But what difference does that make?
Redden	*(leans forward with sympathy and speaks softly)* But don't you think that puts you in the most awful of positions?

Dirsk   I decided not to think about it.

Redden   How did you do that?

Dirsk   It was not my problem. I didn't invent these
            circumstances. I fell into them. I came here early this
            morning, I saw the same sign on the door that everyone
            else saw, and this lady . . . I don't know her name . . .

Redden   Gabi.

Dirsk   Yes, Gabi said that I was just to sit in this room and when
            people entered they would do so as applicants for a job.
            She said she would not tell me about the job because that
            would spoil the purity of the situations – whatever that is,
            because she didn't tell me that either. She told me to listen
            to each person for a few minutes, let them apply for the
            post, and then dismiss them. *(pauses, then rather startled)*
            How do you know Gabi?

Redden   Because I'm her boss.

Dirsk   What?

*From her blouse, Redden pulls out an ID card on a lanyard and brings it
forward so Dirsk can read it.*

Redden   You see. I am the boss of this institution.

Dirsk   I don't understand this.

Redden   I know. But you applied for a job and actually you got it
            first thing. Your job was to interview people for your own
            job, but neither they nor you knew this. You existed in
            absolute ignorance of your context, even though you
            accepted your function and you exercised it – as I
            understand it, with consummate skill. Gabi did select exit
            interviews and you came out with high marks.

Dirsk   Why didn't you tell me?

Redden   Why should we? Your job is simply to function without
            knowing why. If we'd given you a wider purpose, if we'd

explained anything to you, it would have ruined our ability to assess whether you were the man for the job or whether we would have to sack you and get someone else.

Dirsk   So, you're telling me I have the job?

Redden   Yes, that's why I'm here at the end of your very long first day.

Dirsk   But what is my job?

Redden   It is to do what you have been doing.

Dirsk   But now that I know what it is, doesn't that change what I have been doing?

Redden   Only slightly, because each applicant might prove to be better on the job than you and, this being a competitive marketplace, if so, then he or she would get the job.

Dirsk   But how could they do that? I mean, what qualifications would they have that were superior to my own demonstrated qualities?

Redden   Well, if I told you that, then it might persuade you to disallow them a chance – and that would hardly be good business practice on my part, would it? But you being you, if someone exceeded your abilities, then you would probably just vacate your post, don't you think?

Dirsk   Yes, I would have been replaced.

Redden   Indeed.

Dirsk   But to be better than me they would have to know less than me, to be absolutely bewildered, and yet function better than I did with no idea of where I was or what I was doing.

Redden   Correct. That is why you have the job and no one else. And, frankly, I hope you'll keep up the good work and maintain your position.

Dirsk   So I got the job in the first place because when I applied,
           Gabi told me to sit in this room and interview people
           and . . .

Redden   You never asked a single question.

Dirsk   Right, I didn't ask . . .

Redden   . . . a single question, and when she told you to sit in the
           chair you did so right away. And when she told you to
           simply let people apply without knowing what they were
           applying for, you just nodded your head and you said . . .

Dirsk   'I see . . .'

Redden   Yes, you said 'I see.' That impressed us immediately and
           you got the job. *(sits back)* But . . . I confess . . . we were
           and are a bit curious. When you said 'I see', what exactly
           did you see? Was it simply a manner of speaking – which
           some of us think it was – or was it a reference to seeing
           something more deeply, and if so, what was it you thought
           you saw?

Dirsk   My life.

Redden   Your life?

Dirsk   I thought I saw my life.

Redden   Interesting, but . . .

Dirsk   You don't see?

Redden   Ah, Mr Dirsk. You are quite superb at this! I don't see. I
           don't see. Well, let's see, shall we? I see a man who shows
           no sign of anything. You're just a name, a man with a
           name. A man with a mixed name – your given name is
           Hispanic, I think, and your last name seems German or
           Dutch, but it is unclear. So you're a man . . .

Dirsk   . . . without an explanation.

Redden	. . . without an explanation for himself. Yes, good. So I do see something, don't I?
Dirsk	What do you see?
Redden	That you exist in name only but have never asked after your own name and know nothing of it, so when we gave you a job with no meaning but only a function, you saw yourself as the man for the job.
Dirsk	Looking back, yes.
Redden	Yes, looking back.
Dirsk	At the time.
Redden	At the time.
Dirsk	I . . .
Redden	You . . .
Redden and Dirsk	. . . knew nothing.
Dirsk	And now?
Redden	You don't know any more than before, do you?
Dirsk	No, I don't.
Redden	For all the time that has passed and all the people you have met . . .
Dirsk	Some very intense moments.
Redden	Very . . . but you still don't know any more about people, your life, or yourself, do you?
Dirsk	No, I don't.
Redden	That's why this is the perfect job for you.
Dirsk	Because I learn nothing from it?

Apply Within

Redden	Because you're safe. Because life, for all its characters and its devices, for all its diversity and colours, for all its joys and sorrows, doesn't reach you here.
Dirsk	'Apply within.'
Redden	That's what the sign said. *(pauses, looks at him intently)* Do you know where you are?
Dirsk	I'm 'within'?
Redden	Close.
Dirsk	I'm not dead . . . am I?
Redden	No, you're not dead.
Dirsk	The sign said 'Job available, apply within' and I came in and I got the job and now I am inside, within, and I'm safe. I'm not dead. But you asked did I know where I was?
Redden	Yes, do you know where you are?
Dirsk	In your world, then?
Redden	Yes, you're in my world.
Dirsk	Because you are the boss.
Redden	That's right, because I am the boss.
Dirsk	And you know things, but I am ignorant.
Redden	That is exactly true. I know things and you are innocent of what I know.
Dirsk	And that is my job?
Redden	Yes, your job is to be in my world, which I know and you do not, to function 'here' but to know nothing of it.
Dirsk	That way, if I leave – or am sacked – I can't take away your corporate secrets.
Redden	That's a wonderfully inventive way of thinking about where you are.

Dirsk	So the less I know . . .
Redden	The more secure you are . . .
Dirsk	The less I know of myself . . .
Redden	The more of an insider you can become.
Dirsk	And my job will be safe.
Redden	Some would say it's a perfect world.
Dirsk	Because I experience life, yet it doesn't touch me.
Redden	It can't reach you here, but you can see as much of it as you like.
Dirsk	Does the institution have a name?
Redden	It is called many things, but it is not for me to name it.
Dirsk	But it has been named?
Redden	It has been given names but it is more of a location for people. Anyway, it's not important for your purposes. We have to stop now.

Redden gets up, blows Dirsk a kiss, and walks to the door. As she opens it, she turns round.

Oh, do you have any questions before I go?

| Dirsk | Yes. Did you ever know my mother? |
| Redden | No. |

Redden exits and closes the door behind her. Dirsk sits in silence for some seconds, watching the door as if he expects Redden to reappear.

Dirsk   *(very softly)* Next.

The stage lights go out.

Your Object Or Mine?

A brief farce

Cast

Dr Scarf

Mr Wellbird

A psychoanalyst's office, containing a couch with a chair behind it, a comfortable sofa, and two additional chairs with a coffee table between them. There is a desk with family photos on it, a picture of Freud on one wall, and sundry paintings.

Scarf, a well-dressed man in his thirties or forties, is standing at the open door of the office, speaking to his previous patient, who is off-stage.

Scarf   See you next Tuesday at 2.30.

He walks around in circles, lost in thought, then suddenly stops himself, races to his desk and picks up a file, which he now reads out loud, pacing back and forth.

'Dear Dr . . . um . . . blah blah . . . live in Belize, New Mexico, just outside . . .' Belize, New Mexico? Never heard of it! '. . . want to come to see you to talk about my international objects.' What? What does he mean? Jesus . . . I should have read this before . . . I never have time. Just no time. *(pauses)* What does he mean, 'international objects'? *(there is a knock on the door)* Shit. Okay. Collect yourself, doctor!

Scarf opens the door and steps back slightly. Wellbird is in his sixties or possibly seventies. He looks almost like a hobo, but actually he is colourfully adorned in a South-West American outfit: jeans, chequered shirt, and cowhide jacket, on which there is a little flashing light (such as those made by Super Bright Flashing Jewelry). He is carrying a medium-sized black travelling trunk.

Wellbird   Hello. Dr Scarf?

Scarf	Mr Wellbread?
Wellbird	Wellbird. Wellbird.
Scarf	*(standing back, showing Wellbird the way to a chair)* Oh, of course. Well. Well, I don't . . . Of course, Mr . . . *(flustered, he looks at the file)* Wellbird. Do sit down.

They sit down. Scarf drops the file onto the floor to his left. Wellbird puts the trunk on the floor next to his chair. There is a brief pause.

	So, tell me . . . what brings you?
Wellbird	I was online some months ago, and I came across your website, and it was like a revelation. I ran out of the door of my trailer – I live in the desert – and yelled 'Whoopee!' *(he yells this and Scarf is taken aback)* Now I know to whom I can bring my international objects.
Scarf	Your international objects?
Wellbird	Yes, of course. You see, until I saw your website and discovered the fact that you actually had an institute to study international object relations, I thought I could never sort out the problem I was having with my international objects, which just do not relate. I can't figure it out, so I thought I would visit you.
Scarf	*(moving his chair back just a bit)* Sure, sure . . . This makes sense.
Wellbird	Yes. That's why I've come. And I couldn't do it by air or by train, so I drove.
Scarf	You drove?
Wellbird	Well, if I'd flown, I couldn't have trusted that my objects would be okay in the plane. I mean, they could all have been mixed up. And I think even the train wouldn't have been good for them. *(sitting on the edge of his seat, he moves his chair close to Scarf)* Anyway, I drive them around, and that's my experience, and we are all safer for it.

Scarf	You are safer?
Wellbird	Yes. You can't believe how crazy I get when my international objects are jumbled. I . . . well . . . I just sort of lose my mind.
Scarf	You lose your mind?
Wellbird	Well, that's what my neighbours in Taos told me. I have little memory of it, but I solved it by moving out into the desert. There I can look after my objects, and if anything goes wrong I can go crazy, and I don't bother anyone, you know. *(looks at Scarf, who is paralysed and speechless)* So . . . do you want to look?
Scarf	Look?
Wellbird	Yes, would you like to see my objects?
Scarf	See them? *(again moving his chair back a bit)* Is that really necessary? Don't you think we can . . . I mean . . . I think it's best if we talk about them, don't you?
Wellbird	Well, can't we look at them and talk about them at the same time?
Scarf	Yes, I think that's rather what I meant. If we talk about them then we are, so to speak, looking at them.
Wellbird	Oh, Dr Scarf, you are joking!

Wellbird roars with laughter, doubling over. As he recovers, he jerks his chair forwards, even closer to Scarf, and with his right hand he pulls the small coffee table closer to the two of them; it is now facing the audience. Wellbird rather violently knocks a box of tissues off the coffee table, before placing his trunk on the table instead.

> I love your sense of humour. What a joker! I knew you would be a man of wit! Imagine not wanting to look at my objects, but just talking about them!

Wellbird opens the trunk by forcefully unzipping the top, as Scarf stands up, pushing his chair back.

Scarf   Wait a minute! What are you doing?

Wellbird   *(in a more serious tone, somewhat annoyed)* Dr Scarf, come on. I've come all this way, I've booked you for forty-five minutes, and I at least have the right to show you my objects. My INTERNATIONAL objects. Please sit down, you're making me nervous. *(he says this with a sweeping gesture of his hand, and Scarf moves back into his seat)* So . . . this will take a minute.

Wellbird puts the trunk on the floor and carefully removes about fifteen rocks: some small, others large, of different colours and shapes. He places them carefully on the coffee table in what seems to be some kind of order. He is obviously deep in thought, nodding to himself, sometimes shaking his head, sometimes pausing, as if playing a game of chess. This takes at least two minutes, while Scarf simply looks on, nonplussed. After Wellbird has finished arranging his rocks, he looks at Scarf.

     So! What do you think?

Scarf   What do I think?

Wellbird   Of my objects?

Scarf   Uh . . . I . . . Mr Welldread . . .

Wellbird   It's Wellbird.

Scarf   Mr Wellbird . . . I think there is some sort of mistake.

Wellbird   Of course there is, Dr Scarf. Why else do you think I came all this way?

Scarf   No, I mean, I think there's a rather serious mistake taking place here.

Wellbird   You're telling me! Come on, come on. *(gesturing to Scarf encouragingly)* You can figure this out. You study this all the time. Why don't they relate? Something is wrong. It went wrong years ago. They used to be fine according to how I had arranged them, and then one day . . . and I don't know what it was . . . Was there an earthquake? Did

I sleepwalk? Did they disturb one another? But anyway –
and I'm sure you can figure this out – they were never
again in the same order afterwards.

Scarf   Mr Birdwell, I think they are rocks. *(points to them, his*
          hands trembling, while searching Wellbird's face with anxiety)
          I believe . . . they are . . . you know . . . rocks.

Wellbird A man of your intelligence . . . saying they're rocks?
          They're more than rocks! They're objects of differing type
          and shape, of different colours, and they are from around
          the world. *(pointing as he names them)* Afghanistan, China,
          Brazil, Alaska, Maine, Nepal, South Africa . . . *(angry now*
          and increasingly passionate) Do I have to go on? They
          REPRESENT our mother earth and her countries and
          history. They're not rocks, they're objects, and they're all a
          jumble and I can't live without my objects in a proper
          relationship together!

Scarf   I don't quite know how to explain something to you.

Wellbird Go on, try me! *(smiling now, confident he can answer any of*
          Scarf's questions)

Scarf   Um . . . you see . . . the International Institute of Object
          Relations studies what we call 'internal objects'.

Wellbird What?

Scarf   Internal objects.

Wellbird Well, what the hell is an internal object?

Scarf   Well, they are objects that we have inside us. If your
          objects were, so to speak, INSIDE you, then I could in
          some ways be of help to you.

Wellbird Oh, for Christ's sake.

*Suddenly Wellbird picks up a small stone and swallows it (it is in fact a
small cake).*

Scarf	No! No, don't.
Wellbird	Well, you want it inside me. Now it is. How the hell else am I going to make this consultation worth my money? How else can you get an object inside you, if you don't swallow it? So . . . well . . . I don't know how you do this . . . but . . . *(reaches for another stone and opens his mouth)*
Scarf	No! Look. Please wait. *(reaches over and gently takes the stone from Wellbird's hand)* There really is no need for this.
Wellbird	I thought not.
Scarf	Yes, no need.
Wellbird	So, we can talk about my objects without my having to swallow them?
Scarf	Yes, you need not do that.

Scarf pauses and searches Wellbird's face. Then he inhales deeply, looks to the ceiling and speaks a bit like a professor.

	You see, Mr Bridwell . . .
Wellbird	Wellbird.
Scarf	Yes, Wellbird. I . . . that is, we here . . . We study what we call 'internal objects', but actually they do not really exist.
Wellbird	What?
Scarf	They are not actually there, as in they have no substantial matter to them.
Wellbird	What the hell are you talking about?
Scarf	The objects we study are mental. We study how people take in – we call it 'incorporate', or 'introject' – objects from the outside world and hold them inside as internal objects, as mental objects, like an image of a rock, but not actually the rock itself.
Wellbird	And you get paid for this?

Scarf   *(a bit offended)* Yes, of course I do.

Wellbird   Whatever for?

Scarf   Because I help people with their internal objects.

Wellbird   Well, if they don't exist, except in your mind, how the hell could you help anyone with them? What do you do?

Scarf   I talk to them.

Wellbird   Well! *(laughs derisively)* That's a good one! You talk to internal objects! What is this, April Fool's Day? Halloween, maybe . . . ? So . . . how do you talk about internal objects? *(looks around the room somewhat anxiously, as though in a place of potential danger)*

Scarf   I talk to people, you know, about how there are good and bad objects, or how people attack their objects and then can expect retaliations.

Wellbird   *(moving his chair back, clearly alarmed)* Oh really? You . . . you talk to these internal objects that people have lying around inside them . . . You talk to them . . . you talk to them about how they are good or bad and go after people?

Scarf   Roughly speaking, yes.

Scarf now appears more confident. Meanwhile, Wellbird is collecting his stones and rocks and putting them back into his trunk.

            You see, INTERNAL objects start with our relation to the breast – what we call the good and the bad breast, which are engaged in a war with one another, or we with them, or . . .

Wellbird   What breasts? What are you talking about?

Scarf   With our, you know . . . our mother's breasts.

Wellbird   You leave my mother's breasts out of this!

Scarf   No, not YOUR mother's breasts, but OUR mother's breasts . . . What I mean to say . . .

Wellbird	My mother is not your mother.
Scarf	Of course, not actually, but you know, as an INTERNAL OBJECT they are . . . well . . . In a psychological sense, we all share the same idea – er, the same mother. It's a paradigm.

Wellbird picks up his suitcase and walks slowly and anxiously towards the door.

Wellbird	Does anyone know you think like this?
Scarf	Sure, lots of people.
Wellbird	Does anyone know about these 'lots of people' and what they think?
Scarf	Uh . . . well . . . I think . . . well . . . Sometimes . . . it's possible that they don't know so much about . . .
Wellbird	About being chased by our mother's breast that's going to get us because we've done something wrong? Does anyone know you all think like this?
Scarf	I think . . . well, we think . . . We cannot use technical language with the lay . . . er . . . .public, if you know what I mean.
Wellbird	What technical language?
Scarf	Well . . . you know . . . technical . . . like . . .
Wellbird	What, like 'breast'? That's technical?
Scarf	'Bad breast', then.
Wellbird	How can you possibly expect to sort out objects if you go on dreaming about breasts, good, bad, indifferent, or . . . Well! Ah ha! Ah ha! Ha! *(taking heart, as he reaches the door)* Of course. Breasts! Ah ha! Yes. Hah!
Scarf	Hah what?

Wellbird   Well, I know a great breast when I see one, and a bad one, for that matter. So it's knockers you're into, is it, Scarf? And if you happen to say you don't like the set in front of you, you'd better duck – is that it? Well, I'm going! *(opens the door)*

Scarf   Wait!

Wellbird pauses in bewilderment.

     I have an interpretation.

Wellbird   A what?

Scarf   An interpretation.

Wellbird   Of what?

Scarf   Of this. Of THIS . . . of what is happening . . . of you and I . . . of everything.

Wellbird   *(resigned)* Well, get on with it.

Scarf   I think . . . I think . . . *(looking truly lost, but then rising up and pointing his finger at Wellbird)* I think, Wellbird, that you can't get your rocks off!

Wellbird   I certainly can. We're leaving. *(looking triumphant, holding up his suitcase)* My rocks and I are off!

Wellbird exits. Scarf stands in the middle of the room, clears his throat, walks over to the mirror, adjusts his tie, and runs a comb through his hair. He then walks to his desk and reaches for a file.

Scarf   So, let's see . . . who's next?

The lights go out.